THE WAY THINGS HAPPEN

THE WAY THINGS HAPPEN

A STORY IN THREE ACTS

BY

CLEMENCE DANE

LONDON
WILLIAM HEINEMANN LTD

First Published, 1924

Printed in Great Britain by
Woods & Sons, Ltd., London, N.1

Cast of the original production by the ReandeaN Company, at the Ambassadors Theatre, London, February 2nd, 1924:

MRS. FARREN	HAIDÉE WRIGHT
SHIRLEY PRYDE	HILDA BAYLEY
MARTIN FARREN	ROBERT HARRIS
HARNESS	CICELY OATES
MURIEL HANBURY	OLGA LINDO
CHUSSIE HARE	WALTER HUDD
BENNETT LOMAX	LESLIE BANKS
MRS. HANBURY	ADA KING
DR. RODSON	AUSTIN TREVOR
AN OUTSIDE PORTER	ALAN HOWLAND

Produced by BASIL DEAN.

In Memory
Meggie Albanesi

THE PEOPLE OF THE PLAY

In the order of their appearance.

MRS. FARREN.
SHIRLEY PRYDE.
MARTIN FARREN.
HARNESS.
MURIEL HANBURY.
CHUSSIE HARE.
BENNETT LOMAX.
MRS. HANBURY.
DR. RODSON.
AN OUTSIDE PORTER.

THE SCENE, THROUGHOUT THE PLAY, IS THE SITTING ROOM OF A SMALL HOUSE IN THE SUBURBS.

ACT I.—A SATURDAY EVENING IN JUNE.

ACT II.—THE MIDDLE OF THE FOLLOWING MORNING.

ACT III.—*Scene* I. TWO YEARS LATER. AFTERNOON.

        Scene II. THREE WEEKS LATER. AFTERNOON.

B

ACT I.

The curtain rises on the sitting-room of an old cottagey house long since Victorianised and lately suffering still further under jazz cretonnes and a gramophone. It is a comfortable room with a Turkey carpet shabby as the furniture, a couple of easy chairs, half-a-dozen straight-backed ones, a chesterfield, and a solid, oblong dining-table. The Adam mantelpiece is draped in a mantel-border with a bobby fringe and displays a solid marble-cased clock, two wrought-iron candlesticks without any candles, and a pair of photographs in frames. A looking-glass occupies the space between the mantel and the ceiling. On either side of the fireplace hang photographs of Watts' "Love and Life" and "Love and Death." Under one is a Shakespeare "pull off" calendar, and under the other stands a bookshelf filled with classics in Victorian bindings, a complete set of Edna Lyall, and a fair sprinkling of sevenpennies. On the opposite wall stands a mahogany sideboard carrying a dessert dish filled with fruit, and some good silver. Above it hangs Stoddart's "Canterbury Pilgrims" in a yellow mahogany frame. On the same wall, nearer the back of the room, is a door leading to the passage and the front door. Once past this door the smothered room reasserts itself by providing a staircase with a delicately turned hand-rail, which leads to a landing with a bedroom door in sight and a probable second beyond. At the back under this gallery are large wide-open French windows looking on to a tidy moon-lit garden. In the day-time there is a view of fields and low hills, built over at the foot though still possessing green and wooded crests; but at this hour you notice only how blue the twilight shows against the fire-lit walls with their old-fashioned wall papers. Perhaps it is the fire that gives the room, with all its drawbacks, such a welcoming air. A kettle hisses on the hob, and a plate and vegetable dish are set to warm: also slippers, though this last touch, even more than the fire, seems out of keeping with the fine June evening and the bowls of flowers. For flowers are everywhere, beautiful common weeds, the overflow of the distant fields, and SHIRLEY, *even as the curtain goes up, is refilling a jampot full of drooping buttercups and wild parsley (she has run out of vases), from the water jug that is part of the ended meal. Ended so far as* SHIRLEY *and her companion are concerned, for half the white tablecloth has been neatly rolled back; but the other half is still covered by a cloth, and a place has been laid, knife, fork and spoon, with a cold joint and cheese dish in front of it.*

MRS. FARREN *is sitting by the fire in a large invalid chair She is a shrewd yet sweet-looking woman with a thin face, grey hair and an adorable twinkle. She has a low table in front of her with half a pack of cards laid out, and she is busy dealing out the other half. She is a picture of peace-and-quiet and good temper, while* SHIRLEY *on the other hand is restless. She is not content with filling her jampot, but she must pull out and re-arrange one spray after another, all the while casting fidgety glances at the door. This* SHIRLEY *is a girl of twenty or there-abouts. Her figure is hidden in a shapeless, dun-coloured kitchen overall; she is pale, dark-haired, dark-eyed, and not good-looking until she smiles. People generally speak of her as " a queer little thing" and yet she is not so little, is sturdily built indeed, with erect carriage and capable, work-stained hands. She moves deftly, and is obviously efficient, and yet you have the feeling that this efficiency does not come quite naturally to her. She reminds you of a born dreamer who is never allowed a good long sleep : it gives her an air of strain.   Her manner, too, is either so impassive and suppressed as to make you think her stupid, or else as vehement as the little kettle boiling over on the hearth.   But whoever suppresses her it is certainly not* MRS. FARREN, *for the affection between them is evident, even when, as now,* SHIRLEY *is called to order.*

MRS. FARREN. Shirley, the kettle !

SHIRLEY [*rushing to the rescue*]. Oh, I'm sorry !

MRS. FARREN. Take it off !   Why have you got it in here?

SHIRLEY. The kitchen fire's out.   I thought Martin might want some shaving water.

MRS. FARREN. Oh, I see !

SHIRLEY [*going back to her flowers*]. I wish he'd come.   His supper will be all cold.

MRS. FARREN [*dealing out cards*]. He won't notice.

SHIRLEY. I do hate it when he doesn't get a proper meal.   I mean, when one's cooked it carefully—and he'll think I didn't bother.

MRS. FARREN [*counting*]. Four on the three: five on the four— He won't think anything of it one way or the other.

SHIRLEY. That's what— [*she checks herself*].

MRS. FARREN. What's what?   It's bad manners not to finish your sentences.

SHIRLEY. Well—

MRS. FARREN. Queen by the Knave ; King by the Queen—Well ?

SHIRLEY. Don't *you* think Martin's altered since he's engaged ? He's—he's—

MRS. FARREN. Fretty !   He was just the same over his teething. Men don't alter.

SHIRLEY. *I* think being in love ought to make people more unselfish.

MRS. FARREN. Depends whom they're in love with.

SHIRLEY. Do you really like Muriel, Aunt Lucy?

MRS. FARREN. Do I really like measles? But I nursed him through that and I'll nurse him through this, please God!

SHIRLEY. Yes, but—

MRS. FARREN. Why, goodness me, child, you don't suppose I'm going to let my Martin marry Muriel Hanbury, do you?

SHIRLEY. Well, he's twenty-three, and he's got a will of his own.

MRS. FARREN. Well, I'm fifty-three, and he's got the will I gave him. Besides, it's in the cards who Martin is going to marry.

SHIRLEY. Oh, your old cards. [*She turns away. Then, off-handedly*] Is it in the cards, Aunt Lucy? Have you told them lately?

MRS. FARREN. Not since the night he told me he was engaged.

SHIRLEY. But you saw—? You did see—? I don't believe in it, you know.

MRS. FARREN. You haven't got gipsy blood in you.

SHIRLEY. Well, Martin doesn't believe it either, and he has. [*Then, as* MRS. FARREN *quietly continues to shuffle*] Who—who—I mean—Muriel must have been in them—

MRS. FARREN. Oh yes, she was in. But she goes out. I'm getting old, my dear, and feebler than Martin thinks, poor boy—

SHIRLEY [*disturbed by her tone*]. Aunt Lucy!

MRS. FARREN. Oh, you may as well know it. Dr. Matheson served me with preliminary notices six months ago. You needn't tell Martin.

SHIRLEY. But I think he ought to know.

MRS. FARREN. You mind your own business, my dear. If you think I've any intention of dying before I've turned him over to the right woman—

SHIRLEY [*fidgeting with the plates*]. Who—? Have you—? Who will she—?

MRS. FARREN [*flicking an amused look at her*]. She won't be Muriel Hanbury anyway. What are you doing with those dishes?

SHIRLEY [*at the grate*]. It's only the vegetables—to keep them hot for him.

MRS. FARREN. You shouldn't keep things hot for a man till you've been married to him for at least three years—then you should never forget to.

SHIRLEY [*sharply*]. I'm not going to get married.

MRS. FARREN. Mm!

SHIRLEY. Not ever—ever! Oh, I mean it.

MRS. FARREN. It seems to me that Martin's not the only one that's altered lately.

SHIRLEY. Everything's altered. Oh, of course I know it's no business of mine. After all, I'm only a glorified kitchen-maid. Oh yes, I am, Aunt Lucy! You're always a darling to me, but you don't think Muriel hasn't been careful to rub in the difference between us.

MRS. FARREN. Difference? Fiddlesticks! You're both excessively ill-tempered and quarrelsome young women, and the only difference between you is that Muriel Hanbury doesn't know any better and you do. At least you ought to. I brought you up.

SHIRLEY. Yes, that's it. You shouldn't have. I'm not a relation. I hadn't any claim.

MRS. FARREN. Your mother was a dear soul, I couldn't let you straggle up in an orphanage. Besides—[*with her twinkle*] it was good for Martin to have someone to play with.

SHIRLEY [*fiercely*]. I love you! I do love you! But—I'm *not* grateful.

MRS. FARREN. I didn't do it for you. I did it for your mother.

SHIRLEY. No, you didn't! It was that Martin should have some-one to play with.

MRS. FARREN. Well, didn't you enjoy playing with him?

SHIRLEY. I don't think it was fair to let me be—be one of you—to let me forget that I didn't really belong. Don't you see what out-siders think of me? Don't you see what Muriel thinks? A hanger-on.   And yet I do run the place for you, don't I?   I *am* useful.   Oh, it was so jolly, just us three, and now she's turning me out.   She said to me yesterday—

Mrs. Farren.   Muriel?

Shirley.   Who else?   Yes, she said only yesterday, *you* know, drooping her eyes at me—" By the way, *are* you a cousin ? " (Because I call you Aunt, you know.)   And she can't cook or sew or clean or do anything, except powder her nose and fox-trot and make a fool of him.   She does, Aunt Lucy.   You don't see.   She makes him wait on her and give her things, and he spends every penny on her and you know he can't afford it and—oh well, it amuses him and doesn't hurt me, I suppose.   [*Pause.   She stands looking over* Mrs. Farren's *shoulder.   Then*—] Aunt Lucy!

Mrs. Farren.   Well?

Shirley.   Do you truthfully believe in the cards?

Mrs. Farren.   They're as old as—Egypt.   They've told me true things in their time.

Shirley.   But if they tell you what's going to happen, then you're warned and can do differently.   And so they *don't* come true.

Mrs. Farren.   Well, my experience is, if a thing's meant to happen, it will happen.   If it doesn't one way it'll do it another.   The cards don't tell you the way things happen.   They only foretell the happenings.

Shirley.   But suppose now that they said that Martin, for instance, was going to do something foolish—

Mrs. Farren [*sharply*].   Why do you pitch on Martin?

Shirley [*not looking at her*].   Oh, I don't know—why not?

Mrs. Farren.   Only that it's his fortune that I'm telling this moment and—

Shirley [*bending over the cards eagerly*].   Oh, show me!

Mrs. Farren.   There's trouble, Shirley, sure and certain trouble coming to him.

SHIRLEY [*under her breath*]. Trouble? We won't let it. We'll prevent it somehow.

MRS. FARREN. See here! Here's the Knave of diamonds—reversed : that's trouble from a fair man. And all the diamonds are round him : that's money trouble and treachery, and I don't know what all besides. And see here—look at this Queen!

SHIRLEY. I suppose that stands for Muriel.

MRS. FARREN. Muriel's fair. Here's Muriel. Hearts and diamonds are squeezing her out. No, this is the club, the dark woman, and she brings trouble with her—trouble for her and trouble for him. Yet, see here—all the hearts are round her and there's a marriage card between them. Odd, isn't it? [*With a sidelong look of amusement*] Can *you* think of any dark woman?

SHIRLEY [*turning away*]. Oh, it's all such rubbish.

MRS. FARREN [*placidly*]. Well, my dear, fortunes have been raked out of rubbish heaps before now. [*She gathers the cards and shuffles.*]

SHIRLEY [*coming back to the table—abruptly, almost threateningly*]. Tell my fortune!

MRS. FARREN [*teasing her*]. What? When it's all such rubbish. Well, if you like. [*She claps the pack together and holds it out to her*] Cut!

SHIRLEY [*irresolutely*]. No. Don't! I'd rather you didn't. I was only joking. I've got to put on the coffee. [*She takes down the coffee-pot from the sideboard and polishes it with a duster.*] Martin is late. He'll hardly have time to change.

MRS. FARREN. What time are the others coming?

SHIRLEY. They won't be here till nine.

MRS. FARREN. Then I'll get off to bed before they come. Call Harness!

SHIRLEY. They'll only be here for a minute to fetch Martin. They're going on to the pictures—the second house.

MRS. FARREN. They're too noisy for me. I suppose it's the usual half dozen from the office.

SHIRLEY. No, I think it's only Muriel and Mr. Lomax—and Chussie, of course.

MRS. FARREN. Now I like that boy.

SHIRLEY. Chussie? He's not so bad. It's Mr. Lomax—

MRS. FARREN. Knave of Diamonds—hm!

SHIRLEY [*impatiently*]. He's always here.

MRS. FARREN [*apparently busy with her cards*]. Shirley—if Mr. Lomax ever tries to make love to you—

SHIRLEY [*sharply*]. How did you know?

MRS. FARREN [*equally sharply*]. So he has, has he?

SHIRLEY. Oh—nothing to take hold of. At least—I don't know what he's driving at sometimes. I hate men when they get all—excited.

MRS. FARREN. You ought to have told me. I'd have settled it. A married man!

SHIRLEY. What was she like?

MRS. FARREN. The wife? They were separated before we got to know him.

SHIRLEY. Martin told me he's sure it wasn't Mr. Lomax' fault.

MRS. FARREN. Martin's geese are all swans. It's so trying.

SHIRLEY. I wish they weren't such friends.

MRS. FARREN. It'll wear off. It's never any good trying to stop these enthusiasms. Hark, isn't that Martin at the gate?

SHIRLEY. Aunt Lucy, one step among fifty! [*The latch key turns in the lock and the door opens.*]

MRS. FARREN. I told you so.

> MARTIN *enters, as usual, at full speed. He is a tall gipsyish boy of twenty-three, well set up, with quick gestures and an impetuous delivery. He takes life so seriously that, without being bad-tempered, he has acquired a permanent frown which, together with a down-*

right, impatient manner, flusters SHIRLEY *and makes*
MRS. FARREN *laugh. These foibles apart he has,
for 1923, unusually nice manners. He obviously and
sincerely loves his mother quite half as much as she loves
him. He is scrupulously careful of her comfort and,
when he thinks of it, is kind and affectionate to* SHIRLEY.
*But she is so much a part of his life that, unless he needs
something done for him, he is apt to forget that she has
any separate existence.*

MARTIN. Well, Mother dear! Hullo, Shirley! [SHIRLEY *gives him
a little smile as she goes out.*]

MRS. FARREN. You're late, my son!

MARTIN. Lomax kept me. Overtime as usual. O God, how
I do hate the office! Here, catch! [*He puts down the large
parcel on a side table and flings the other deftly into his mother's lap.*]

MRS. FARREN [*unwrapping the posy and smelling it*]. Sweet!
But you should spend your pennies on Muriel.

MARTIN. Oh, I've got these for Muriel. [*He unwraps the larger
parcel and displays a magnificent spray of orchids.*]

MRS. FARREN. Martin, you extravagant boy.

MARTIN [*with a wry smile*]. Now, don't you begin!

MRS. FARREN. Dreadful! Oh, it reminds me of your father. He
was just the same.

MARTIN. Extravagant? [*Then, suddenly conceding the point
with—*] I don't mean to, you know, but when I get into a shop—
Oh, what's ten shillings? She likes 'em.

MRS. FARREN. These cost more than ten shillings. I thought you
were trying to save, my dear.

MARTIN. Oh, good Lord, I've skinflinted enough these last six
months. And then Chussie always chipping in with his beastly
greenhouse stuff. Hang for a penny, hang for a pound! What's
twenty-five shillings?

MRS. FARREN. Twenty-five shillings, my son.

MARTIN. I know. I didn't mean to spend it either. Mother—that a fact about Father—extravagant?

MRS. FARREN [*without expression*]. He would have what he wanted.

MARTIN. I suppose it's that. It feels like that sometimes—as if there were two people in me, tugging different ways. Mother?

MRS. FARREN. Yes, my son?

MARTIN. What does this place cost to run?

MRS. FARREN [*lifting her eyebrows*]. Well, there's my four hundred —and what you pay in—our total expenses are about six. Shirley's very economical.

MARTIN. We couldn't do it on less, could we?

MRS. FARREN. Well, I suppose we could if we had to. Why?

MARTIN. I was just wondering.

MRS. FARREN. Martin, come here! [*He goes across to her and she looks at him intently.*]

MARTIN [*whimsically*]. It's no good, Mother, my shoes aren't wet and I had an excellent lunch.

MRS. FARREN [*stating a fact*]. You're worried about something.

MARTIN [*quickly*]. Me? No, I'm not. I swear I'm not. I've got nothing to be worried about.

MRS. FARREN [*with the same intent look*]. I can stand any shock you give me, Martin, even if I have got a heart.

MARTIN [*kissing her*]. Bless her! Old fusser, isn't she?

> HARNESS *enters : a burly elderly woman, clean but not too tidy, with a pleasant stupid face. She is capless and her costume, slate-coloured blouse, black skirt dipping at the back, coarse bibless apron, all spell 'daily help': and that indeed she was before the war when the* FARRENS *kept 'three maids, cook and boot-boy.' But she has 'slept in' for some*

years now, and has become a part of the small household,
SHIRLEY'S *stand-by, and a comfort to* MRS. FARREN.

HARNESS. Miss Shirley said you were ready, Ma'am.

MRS. FARREN. Oh yes! [*With a tiny sigh*] Well, good-night, my son. Enjoy yourself!

MARTIN [*injured*]. Aren't you waiting till Muriel comes?

MRS. FARREN [*smiling*]. I daresay she can get along without me.

MARTIN [*very serious*]. Well, I don't know—I think she'll be hurt.

MRS. FARREN. There's Shirley to look after you all. [SHIRLEY *re-enters quietly.*]

MARTIN [*dissatisfied*]. Oh yes, there's Shirley. [*He goes with his mother to the stairs.*]

HARNESS [*helping her*]. That's it, Ma'am! [*They go up the stairs.*]

MARTIN. Any hot water in my room, Harness?

SHIRLEY. No, it's here.

MARTIN. Oh, right! [*He takes the jug from her and makes for the stairs.*]

SHIRLEY [*anxiously*]. Oh, Martin, won't you just have time for a mouthful? I've kept it hot.

MARTIN. No, thanks.

SHIRLEY. Oh, but Martin—

MARTIN [*waving her aside*]. I don't want any. I couldn't touch any.

SHIRLEY. Did you get something out?

MARTIN [*irritably*]. I tell you I didn't want anything. Do you suppose I could bother my head— [*Then, at a tangent*] I say, you're not going to leave the table in this mess, are you, for when Muriel comes?

SHIRLEY. No, of course not! I'll see to it while you dress. [*Then, as he moves aimlessly about the room*] If you're going to dress, old man, you'll have to hurry.

MARTIN [*stopping once more on his way to the stairs*]. Did you put my things out?

SHIRLEY [*clearing rapidly*]. They're on your bed.

MARTIN [*gloomily*]. Not that it matters much. Precious little more evening dress for me that I can see. [*Muttering*] More like broad arrows.

SHIRLEY [*arrested, the tray in her hands*]. What? Oh, Martin what's the matter?

MARTIN. Oh, don't bother me!

SHIRLEY [*abandoning the tray and going to him*]. But Martin— old man—?

MARTIN [*finding her intense concern difficult to resist*]. I'm worried to death, Shirley! I tell you I'm worried to death. You don't know what I've been through. [*For an instant you think the whole story is coming out, but no, he changes his mind*] Did you get on to the laundry about that shirt?

SHIRLEY [*stricken*]. Martin, I'm most awfully sorry. It just got itself forgotten.

MARTIN [*it is a relief to him to flare*]. I don't know what it is about this house, but you never can depend on anyone.

SHIRLEY [*timidly*]. You might tell me—

MARTIN [*sullen again*]. You'll know soon enough. It's the end of everything.

SHIRLEY. Does your mother—?

MARTIN [*quickly: he is, all through the scene, torn between his need for secrecy and his habit of confiding in* SHIRLEY]. Yes, that's it. It's Mother. You needn't think I care for myself.

SHIRLEY. Does Muriel—?

MARTIN. Do you suppose I'd tell this sort of thing to Muriel?

SHIRLEY. But what sort of thing, Martin? Oh, what?

MARTIN. At the office. I'm in the most awful hole. I don't know which way to turn.

SHIRLEY. It's not that receipt?

MARTIN [*tense*]. What do you know about that receipt?

SHIRLEY. Why, Martin, you told me yourself the other night when I found you turning the schoolroom upside down. You said you'd mislaid it—a receipt for bearer bonds.

MARTIN [*relaxing*]. Did I? I'd forgotten. Well, it didn't turn up.

SHIRLEY. Have you told them at the office?

MARTIN. No.

SHIRLEY. Well, of course it's most unfortunate. But they can't do much more than row you for carelessness, can they?

MARTIN [*miserably*]. You wouldn't think so, would you?

SHIRLEY. Well then, don't get yourself into such a state.

MARTIN. It's easy to say that.

SHIRLEY [*struck by his manner*]. Martin, there's nothing really wrong? You haven't done anything?

MARTIN [*evasively*]. I'll be all right if I can find that paper. [*Breaking out*] Oh, hunt about again, old thing, for God's sake! Oblong envelope—broken seal—stiff blue paper.

SHIRLEY. I've searched the house thoroughly.

MARTIN. I know. All the same, go on looking, Shirley! A lot hangs on it.

SHIRLEY. Martin, won't you tell me all about it?

MARTIN [*recklessly*]. I'll tell you this—if I can't find it I'll throw myself under the nearest train.

SHIRLEY [*terrified*]. Martin, don't talk like that.

MARTIN. There's no way out that I can see. [*Harking back*] As for telling Muriel—

SHIRLEY. She's engaged to you, Martin.

MARTIN. She's so—so sensitive—so highly strung. One can't worry her with things. I can't explain it to you.

SHIRLEY. There oughtn't to be anything to explain.

MARTIN. You don't understand a woman like Muriel.

SHIRLEY [*queerly*]. I'm a woman, Martin.

MARTIN. What's that got to do with it? [*Then, as the bell goes, fussing.*] There, that's the crowd. I knew I shouldn't be ready. I told you not to keep me.

SHIRLEY. You're not fit to see anyone. Let me put them off.

MARTIN. Put them off! On the doorstep! Muriel! For goodness sake, Shirley, pull yourself together! [*He dashes upstairs, the jug of water in his hand, as the bell rings again.*]

HARNESS [*entering*]. Shall I answer the door, Miss?

SHIRLEY. No. [*She unbuttons her overall and pulls it hastily off, revealing a very simple but becoming little " semi-evening " frock, and says, as she goes to the outer door*] Here, take this! [*She tosses* HARNESS *the overall.*] And Harness, tell Mrs. Farren I'll come up as soon as I can. [*She disappears and you hear a murmur of voices.*]

HARNESS [*calling after her benevolently*]. Oh, I'll see to her, Miss! You enjoy yourself for once. [*She lumbers up the stairs as* SHIRLEY *returns.*]

SHIRLEY [*to those behind her*]. Did I keep you waiting? I'm so sorry, but with only one servant—

> MURIEL HANBURY *flounces into the room, with* CHUSSIE HARE, *obviously as usual, in attendance.* CHUSSIE *is a red-haired good-tempered boy of twenty-three or so, with big hands and feet which he shuffles when life is difficult. He wears a dinner jacket.* MURIEL *is about his age and extremely pretty. She is of the new flimsy type, slender, graceful, flat-chested, with bright hard eyes, short nose, and full pouting lips. When she smiles she shows pretty little even cat's teeth. Her fair hair is waved and bandaged, her fine complexion obscured by powder and lip salve, her finger tips glitter with nail polish. She has a sort of petulant charm that makes life pleasant*

for her. She bores grown men, but as many women like as dislike her, and there is hardly a boy of her acquaintance who does not imagine himself in love with her. She is in full evening dress, a pink dress with more flutter than cut to it, and flings off a white furred cloak and an embroidered shawl as she enters.

MURIEL [*languidly*]. I can't think how you manage. But, of course, you're quite a cook, aren't you?

CHUSSIE. Oh yes, Martin's always full of her efforts.

MURIEL. Shut up, Chussie! [*To* SHIRLEY] How do you manage about your hands?

SHIRLEY [*stretching out a hand and examining it*]. How do you mean?

MURIEL [*putting hers beside it*]. Oh, I see, you don't. It must save an awful lot of trouble.

SHIRLEY [*unruffled*]. Will you have some cigarettes? Will you help yourselves while I get the coffee? Martin's coming in a minute. [*She goes out.*]

CHUSSIE [*who has watched the little scene in some discomfort*] Look here, Muriel, what have you got your knife into Shirley Pryde for?

MURIEL [*lighting her cigarette*]. Oh, she's too good to live. She bores me.

CHUSSIE. I think she's a jolly nice little thing. Anyway—in her own house—

MURIEL. Her own house! My dear boy, she's no relation of the Farren's. She's a pick-me-up of the old lady's.

CHUSSIE. I didn't know that.

MURIEL. No. To hear Martin talk she might be his sister.

CHUSSIE. If he treats her as his sister I can't think what you object to.

MURIEL. She puts ideas into his head. The dear darling thing really imagines that I'm going to settle down to a sort of scratch

c

matrimony with his mother and his cousins and his aunts, on three hundred a year.   Not while I've got a type-writer.

CHUSSIE. I can't think what you ever got yourself engaged to him for.

MURIEL. I thought it might be amusing to slum a little.   The new poor are as picturesque as the old poor and they don't drop their aitches.   Did you ever see such a house—not touched since 1880 !

CHUSSIE. Muriel, are you at the same old game ?

MURIEL [*demurely*]. Haven't the faintest idea what you're talking about.

CHUSSIE. D'you mean you're not going to marry him ?

MURIEL. Oh yes, if he makes it worth my while.

CHUSSIE. I'd make it worth your while, for that matter !

MURIEL. You couldn't, Chussie, you're too pink and white.   You'll never give anyone thrills down their back.

CHUSSIE. Oh, is that what he does ?

MURIEL. It's when he loses his temper.   You haven't got one.

CHUSSIE. There's not room for two where you live, Muriel.   We've all found that out, all your friends and relations.

MURIEL. Martin hasn't—yet.   It's going to be thrilling.

CHUSSIE. What is ?

MURIEL. Trial of strength.

CHUSSIE. What are you up to ?

MURIEL [*viciously*]. I'm going to out that girl.

CHUSSIE [*uncomfortably*]. I knew something was up !

MURIEL. She's like a periwinkle in its shell.   I'm looking for the pin.

CHUSSIE [*outraged*]. I don't know why I bother about you.   You're a little cat.

MURIEL [*she is sitting on the edge of his chair by now : her hand is amusing itself with his buttonhole*]. Chussie, darling, help me find a pin. [*He glances at her, disarmed : then gets up and shakes himself like a dog coming out of a pond.*]

CHUSSIE [*angrily*]. Shut up, Muriel !

MURIEL [*serenely*]. Now you really *are* behaving like Martin.

CHUSSIE. What's all this fuss about how Martin behaves ? I don't see anything so particular about Martin.

MURIEL. It isn't what he does. It's the way he looks at you.

CHUSSIE [*melting*]. I'll look at you fast enough if that's all you want.

MURIEL. All ? Hm ! All I want from you, Chussie dear !

CHUSSIE. You'll make me lose *my* temper in a minute.

MURIEL. That's better ! Now flash your eyes at me and scowl ! *Comme ça !*

CHUSSIE [*angrily*]. Look here, Muriel—

MURIEL [*enjoying herself*]. That's it ! You're getting the knack.

CHUSSIE. For two pins I'd—

MURIEL [*wickedly*]. *He* does.

CHUSSIE. Does what ? [*Martin runs downstairs and sweeps up his orchids as he goes to* MURIEL.]

MURIEL [*lazily*]. Here, Martin ! Come and show him !

MARTIN. Look here, darling, I got you these.

MURIEL [*as he kisses her*]. There you are, Chussie ! That's how it's done. Now you go and practise ! I daresay Miss Pryde would —understudy !

CHUSSIE. Oh, stow it, Muriel !

MURIEL [*languishing*]. Oh, Martin, I'm so bored. Can't we start ?

MARTIN. Where's Lomax ?

CHUSSIE. Not turned up yet.

MURIEL. Well then, turn on the gramophone ! [CHUSSIE *begins to fiddle with it.*]

MARTIN [*looking about him, fussing*]. I say—no one here to look after you ! Where's Shirley ? Won't you have coffee or something ?

[*Calling*] Shirley! Look here, I say, Shirley, it's too bad— [*He disappears.*]

CHUSSIE [*awkwardly*]. Er—Muriel—don't joke like that before Shirley, will you? It—er—she wouldn't understand—

MURIEL. No, I don't suppose she's ever been kissed in her life—or ever will be!

CHUSSIE. Well, as I said before, she's a jolly nice girl and—

MURIEL [*close to him*]. And as *I* said before—" Go and practise!"

CHUSSIE [*catching her by the waist*]. I will too, you little devil! [*He kisses her.*]

MURIEL [*sparkling*]. Chussie! I'm surprised at you! [SHIRLEY *enters with a coffee tray and sees them:* MARTIN, *following, does not.*]

CHUSSIE [*stricken*]. Look here, I say—I'm most awfully sorry! I didn't mean—I mean I thought—

MURIEL [*sweetly*]. You thought it was Miss Pryde, didn't you, Chussie dear! Come along, Martin! [*She floats up to him, he catches her and swings her into a dance.*]

SHIRLEY [*going uncompromisingly up to* CHUSSIE]. What did she mean?

CHUSSIE. Er—well—I say, let me give you some coffee!

MURIEL [*in the doorway*]. What's the matter with your step to-night, Martin? It's heavy.

MARTIN. Is it, dear? Well, to tell you the truth, I'm depressed.

MURIEL. Then you'll bore me, I warn you, and I shall dance with Chussie.

MARTIN [*stopping in the dance*]. Muriel!

MURIEL. Oh, don't stop!

MARTIN. Muriel, if I were—lamed—one day, and couldn't take you to dances any more—?

MURIEL [*swinging him into the dance again*]. I should dance with Chussie! [*Her pretty laugh bubbles up afresh as they dance out*

*through the French windows and are seen dimly passing to and fro
on the lawn.*]

SHIRLEY [*almost with a wail*]. Oh, she *is* pretty !

CHUSSIE [*uncomfortably*]. Martin's not a bit himself to-night is he?

SHIRLEY [*frightened*]. Have you noticed it too ?

CHUSSIE [*awkwardly*]. I say, you know—only fooling with Muriel—
known her all my life. You don't think he minded ?

SHIRLEY [*relieved*]. Oh, that ! [*Then, uncompromisingly*] I
should have, if I'd been him.

CHUSSIE. Oh, come !

SHIRLEY [*disdainfully*]. I don't see how she can!

CHUSSIE. Look here, I'm not infectious !

SHIRLEY [*with quick pretty apology*]. I don't mean you, specially,
but—

CHUSSIE. But what? [SHIRLEY *shrugs her shoulders.*] But what?
There's no harm in a kiss !

SHIRLEY [*cornered*]. Well, I'd keep mine for the man I was going
to marry. That's what I'd do !

CHUSSIE. I say, you're pretty average straight-laced for 1923 !

SHIRLEY. Well, you made me say it ! [*She looks at him with a
funny little maternal smile as she turns away to the mantel-piece*] I'm
sorry I can't find you a partner too.

CHUSSIE [*following her*]. Well—er— [*He holds out his hands*]
Couldn't you ? What about it ?

SHIRLEY [*pulling down the by-pass of the gas*]. Me? I don't
dance.

CHUSSIE [*lighting the other burner*]. Why not ?

SHIRLEY. Oh—flat feet.

CHUSSIE. Rot! I've seen you run. Come on !

SHIRLEY. I've never learnt. I truly don't know how.

CHUSSIE. Try !

SHIRLEY [*obstinately*]. No !

CHUSSIE. Look here, you know, you're weird! that's what you are, you're weird! Old Lomax is quite right.

SHIRLEY [*stiffening*]. Does Mr. Lomax say that?

CHUSSIE. Oh, he doesn't! Quite the other way! It was the night Muriel told us that she and Martin were engaged. It amused old Lomax no end.

SHIRLEY. Why?

CHUSSIE. Lord knows! And then he began talking about you—said it took a man of experienced taste to appreciate you. He said you were like still champagne.

SHIRLEY [*coldly*]. I don't know if Mr. Lomax always means to be impertinent, but I know he always is.

CHUSSIE. Oh, he didn't mean any harm. He thinks an awful lot of you.

SHIRLEY. He gives me the creeps.

CHUSSIE. Well, you'd better tell him so. He's turning up to-night. A final bust!

SHIRLEY [*as the gramophone stops*]. What?

MURIEL [*in the doorway with* MARTIN]. I say, isn't Lomax here yet?

CHUSSIE. I was just saying we were only waiting for him.

MARTIN. I told him nine.

CHUSSIE. What's the use of hanging about? He can come on afterwards. Shirley can tell him.

MURIEL [*sweetly*]. Oh, aren't you coming, Miss Pryde? Well of course, the evening's spoiled!

MARTIN [*casually*]. Oh, we couldn't both leave Mother.

SHIRLEY [*impassively, to* MURIEL]. Is this your cloak?

MARTIN [*quietly, to* SHIRLEY]. I say, don't go to bed! I may want to talk to you. [*He follows* MURIEL *and* CHUSSIE.]

SHIRLEY. All right! [*Then, calling after them cheerfully*] Enjoy yourselves!

CHUSSIE [*in charge of* MURIEL]. Don't you worry! [*The two disappear.*]

SHIRLEY [*to* MARTIN *at the door, in another voice*]. Martin!

MARTIN [*turning impatiently*]. Yes? What? They're waiting.

SHIRLEY [*timidly*]. Oh, it was only—cheer up, old man!

MARTIN [*shrugging gloomily*]. Oh—*that!* [*He turns to go.*]

SHIRLEY [*her hand flutters towards him*]. There'll be a way out, whatever it is. I feel it!

MARTIN [*turning back to her with one of his sudden impulsive gestures, his secret on his lips*]. Oh, Shirley—

MURIEL [*outside*]. Come along, Martin! Martin!

MARTIN [*recollecting himself*]. Oh—of course! [*He hurries out.*]

SHIRLEY [*clenching her hand*]. Damn that girl!

> BENNETT LOMAX, *who has been seen for a moment hovering by the window, has by this time slipped into the room. He is under forty, tall, fair, smooth, not bad-looking; but against the group of fresh, assured youngsters he strikes you as older than he is, flat and dull and tired. He is not too well bred and knows it: indeed he is one of those people who are always imagining themselves un-welcome and resenting it, and so his manner is half bullying, half timid. He has learned that unless he takes what he wants he will go without and so he is ever on the sway, as one may imagine the beggars in the street must be, between his hungers and his decencies. The right woman would see all this and be sorry for him, perhaps heal him; but in this play, at least, there is no such woman.*
>
> *He stands by the staircase watching* SHIRLEY *with a not too pleasant smile as she turns back into the room.*

LOMAX. That's rather strong, isn't it? What's Muriel been doing? [*He laughs openly as* SHIRLEY *starts and backs away from him.*]

SHIRLEY. Mr. Lomax? Why, they've all been waiting for you.

LOMAX. Yes, haven't they—amazingly patient? I thought they'd never go.

SHIRLEY. Aren't you going to the theatre with them?

LOMAX. Well, as a matter of fact, I wanted a little talk with you, and so—

SHIRLEY. I'm afraid I can't wait, Mr. Lomax! I have to put Mrs. Farren to bed. It—it's Harness's evening out.

LOMAX. Funny! I saw a light in the kitchen. [SHIRLEY *flushes. He looks at her, then he says, with that touch of familiarity with which she finds it so difficult to deal*] You shouldn't tell fibs, you know! It's inartistic of you. It doesn't suit your type. It's just as if you wore your hair as Muriel does—you know—stuck in at the side on a prong.

SHIRLEY [*idly*]. Oh, pin curls!

LOMAX [*coming closer*]. Yes. Don't wear moral pin curls, Shirley! It spoils you for me.

SHIRLEY [*shortly*]. Their seats are in the first circle. Good-night, Mr. Lomax!

LOMAX. Ah, that's more natural. But you're not going. [*He bars the way.*]

SHIRLEY [*indignantly*]. Mr. Lomax, what's the matter with you?

LOMAX [*softly*]. Why, mayn't one say good-bye to an old friend?

SHIRLEY [*brightening too visibly*]. Good-bye?

LOMAX. Didn't Martin tell you? I'm going away. They're making me head of their new branch. The Argentine. Only settled in the last few days. Start to-morrow. [*With point*] I wonder Martin didn't tell you.

SHIRLEY [*relenting : after all he'll be gone to-morrow*]. He's been rather worried.

LOMAX. So I've thought.

SHIRLEY. I expect he won't like losing you. And yet—[*forgetting him*] it's a good thing for Martin.

LOMAX. Yes, he ought to get my place.

SHIRLEY. I didn't mean that.

LOMAX. £500 a year. He can get married on £500 a year, he and Muriel. Yes, a very good thing for Martin—if he gets it.

SHIRLEY [*lifting her head*]. He's next on the list.

LOMAX [*colourlessly*]. Yes.

SHIRLEY [*sharply*]. Why shouldn't he get it?

LOMAX. Why not, indeed?

SHIRLEY [*a step nearer*]. What do you mean?

LOMAX [*quietly*]. If his record is blameless there's no reason why he shouldn't get it.

SHIRLEY [*with a stamp of her foot*]. Mr. Lomax!

LOMAX. Miss Shirley!

SHIRLEY [*hotly*]. I don't understand you. It's as if you were hinting— What have you come here for? Why aren't you with the others? Why do you come and tell me you're going away—me, specially? What has it got to do with me? What—what are you up to?

LOMAX. I like you, Shirley! You're so quick.

SHIRLEY. My name's Shirley Pryde.

LOMAX. It suits you.

SHIRLEY. Good-night, Mr. Lomax!

LOMAX. Good-night, Shirley Pryde!

SHIRLEY [*she gets as far as the door, then hesitates and turns*]. Mr. Lomax—[*he smiles*] I think—if you said that sort of thing to other people about Martin—about Mr. Farren—in that tone—you would get into trouble.

LOMAX. Ah, but I'm going away to-morrow.

SHIRLEY. Nobody could have a finer record than Martin! To join at seventeen—in the last offensive—wounded—his place offered him! And now he's worked himself up—it's sheer jealousy!

LOMAX. Call it that! May I smoke? [*She nods, not thinking,*

*and as he lights his cigarette, comes slowly back across the room to
him.*]

SHIRLEY. Mr. Lomax, there's nothing *wrong*, is there?

LOMAX. What should be wrong in this best of all possible—

SHIRLEY [*irritated*]. Oh, don't!   At the office?

LOMAX. I haven't heard of anything.

SHIRLEY [*closer still : her little hands beginning to work*]. I
mean—over Martin?   There's nothing wrong with Martin?

LOMAX [*smiling*]. What should be wrong with Martin?

SHIRLEY [*squaring herself for a tussle*]. Look here, Mr. Lomax—!

LOMAX [*his eyes on her*]. Willingly, Shirley!

SHIRLEY. I want to talk to you.

LOMAX. That's new, but very pleasant.

SHIRLEY [*awkwardly*]. No, no, I didn't mean—I mean—I want
to talk to you about Martin.

LOMAX. Our dear Martin!

SHIRLEY [*with an eager softening into friendliness*]. Yes, you are
fond of him, aren't you?   You are a friend of his?

LOMAX. Isn't that your principal objection to me?

SHIRLEY [*very much a schoolgirl*]. Oh—I—I don't put it like
that.   [*Then in a rush*] Oh, of course I've never pretended I've
thought you were *good* for him.   I don't mean anything rude, Mr.
Lomax, only of course you can go about and do things—money makes
such a difference—and then Martin wants to do the same, and—
and— Oh, you know what I mean.

LOMAX. Oh, I know!—" Bring us not into temptation and deliver
us—from the evil one!" as the Revised Version hath it.

SHIRLEY [*with a tiny flash of amusement*]. What do you know
about revised versions?

LOMAX [*responding*]. Can't the devil cite Scripture for his purpose?

SHIRLEY. Oh, I didn't say that!

LOMAX [*with a certain wistfulness*]. You'd much rather it were the devil, wouldn't you, Shirley? You don't think much of me, do you?

SHIRLEY. Oh, what does it matter what I think of you?

LOMAX [*significantly*]. It might matter.

SHIRLEY [*not understanding, persuasively*]. Oh, Mr. Lomax, I wish you'd listen.

LOMAX. I love listening to you, Shirley.

SHIRLEY [*bearing with it impatiently*]. No, but look here! Martin's been talking to me and—Mr. Lomax, I'm rather worried. Can't you—couldn't you—I don't want to interfere, you know, but—there *is* something wrong, isn't there?

LOMAX. Well, as far as that goes— Come and sit down and I'll tell you all about it.

SHIRLEY. I'm all right here. [*Pause*] Go on, Mr. Lomax!

LOMAX [*a bullying note has crept into his voice*]. Come and sit down! [*She looks at him a moment, then she sits down quietly at the other end of the sofa*] Now, there's nothing to be frightened about—

SHIRLEY [*sharply*]. I'm not frightened.

LOMAX. But the fact is—Martin's been unwise.

SHIRLEY [*with one of her flashes*]. I think it was up to you not to let him.

LOMAX [*shrugging*]. Am I his keeper?

SHIRLEY. You're his intimate friend.

LOMAX. Some people are born extravagant.

SHIRLEY [*sharply*]. That's only since he got engaged.

LOMAX. Ah, you don't like Muriel.

SHIRLEY. I like her very much indeed, Mr. Lomax. I think she's charming.

LOMAX. Very pretty, isn't she?

SHIRLEY. Very pretty.

LOMAX. In those white furs, for instance—

SHIRLEY. That Martin—[*she stops herself*].

LOMAX. That Martin gave her—very pretty indeed! Have you any idea what they cost?

SHIRLEY. Martin had something on at Lingfield. He told me so. He won a lot.

LOMAX. Did he tell you what he won at Newmarket?

SHIRLEY. What did he win?

LOMAX. He didn't. He lost. He got rather badly into debt. He had to go to a friend to help him out.

SHIRLEY. You helped him?

LOMAX. I helped him.

SHIRLEY. Why?

LOMAX. Why not?

SHIRLEY [*slowly*]. I don't think somehow that you do things for nothing. [*He laughs, half flattered.*] How much did you lend him?

LOMAX. I? I don't waste good money on a young fool's betting debts.

SHIRLEY. No. I thought not.

LOMAX. But I helped him all the same though he doesn't know it.

SHIRLEY. Did you? [*Softening*] That was nice of you. How did you help him?

LOMAX [*significantly*]. I just shut my eyes.

SHIRLEY. How did that help him?

LOMAX. Well, Shirley, how do you suppose it helped him?

SHIRLEY [*with a little uneasy laugh*]. I can't think.

LOMAX. Try!

SHIRLEY [*slowly*]. Are you trying to make out—to make me believe that Martin took money?

LOMAX. Not money.

SHIRLEY. I should think not indeed! Martin a thief!

LOMAX. Call him a borrower. As a matter of fact—he's taken some bonds—bearer bonds.

SHIRLEY. What for?

LOMAX. Raised money on them. The coupons won't be needed till July. He's got another two months. He's obviously reckoning on making good his losses by then. If he redeems them and puts them back nobody'll be the wiser. They're slack in the office. Don't look so shocked. He's not the first scared youngster to grab at a chance.

SHIRLEY. Oh, I don't believe you!

LOMAX. Ask him then.

SHIRLEY. I won't believe it. Martin! It's—it's awful!

LOMAX [*with real feeling, reminiscent*]. It's being in a corner that's awful. You get so desperate. You don't know what you do. You needn't be hard on him. I tell you, I know. I could tell you things in my own life— [*Awkwardly*] Some time, I'll tell you, Shirley. Shirley, I could talk to you—

SHIRLEY [*absorbed, only half attending*]. Oh, what do you matter? It's Martin.

LOMAX. Thank you for your—gentleness. [*He rises.*]

SHIRLEY [*swiftly*]. I didn't mean—I'm sorry— Oh, I'm sorry!

LOMAX [*roughly*]. Yes, I daresay you will be to-morrow. Good-bye! [*He turns away.*]

SHIRLEY [*alarmed, hurriedly*]. Mr. Lomax! Mr. Lomax! What's that? I wasn't rude, was I? I didn't mean to be. I'm only—very troubled. To-morrow? What do you mean—to-morrow?

LOMAX. I shan't be able to start to-morrow, that's all.

SHIRLEY. But you said you were—

LOMAX. I've changed my mind.

SHIRLEY. Why?

LOMAX. I've a certain paper to hand over to headquarters.

SHIRLEY. What paper?

LOMAX. A receipt for bearer bonds.

SHIRLEY. The paper he lost—you found it?

LOMAX. The fool had it in his desk.

SHIRLEY [*contemptuously*]. Oh, so you went prying to his desk like a thief?

LOMAX. Like Martin.

SHIRLEY. How dare you!

LOMAX. It's true.

SHIRLEY. Oh!

LOMAX. But I'll admit it—I was glad to trip him. No malice you know, but—it was my chance.

SHIRLEY [*fiercely*]. It was you from the first. You set him on those ways.

LOMAX. All's fair in love, Shirley. It was my chance!

SHIRLEY. I don't know what you mean.

LOMAX. You know exactly what I mean. Shirley, have you never been jealous?

SHIRLEY [*stumbling*]. There's no cause. Nobody cares about me. I'm not the sort of girl people fall in love with.

LOMAX. That's deviltry, to rope me in.

SHIRLEY [*shrinking from him*]. Oh, don't! I hate it. Oh, please! What's the good of behaving like this?

LOMAX. I suppose you think you can torment me as you like because I can't ask you to marry me.

SHIRLEY [*badgered beyond endurance*]. I never thought of such a thing. I think you might be decent to me. I've got to be decent to you because of—

LOMAX. Because of what you want to get out of me. Is that it?

SHIRLEY [*suddenly making up her mind, very sweetly and earnestly*]. Mr. Lomax, you'll give me that paper—I know you will. You couldn't use it. You couldn't be such a—so heartless—

LOMAX. Yes, it would be the end of Martin, wouldn't it?

SHIRLEY [*piteously*]. Oh, does it *amuse* you to try and frighten me?

LOMAX [*watching her*]. It frightens me to think of the position Martin will find himself in next week if we—if you and I—

SHIRLEY. Yes—if we—?

LOMAX. Don't take steps to help him.

SHIRLEY. But isn't that what I'm begging you to do—to help him?

LOMAX [*shortly*]. It's you who can help him, not I.

SHIRLEY. I? Why, I'd do anything. You know I would. But I haven't any money, Mr. Lomax. I haven't a farthing. He should have it if I'd got it, he and his mother.

LOMAX [*more gently*]. Your pennies won't help them, you funny little thing. You're very fond of them, aren't you, of Martin and his mother.

SHIRLEY. I was in an orphanage for six months, you know. Oh, they were very kind. But—such a lot of us—and no one to belong to. I know how a stray dog feels when it's followed someone home and isn't turned out. You can't understand, of course,—but I tell you—such a stray dog—it has a *passion* for the people who let it stay. Mrs. Farren says she's adopted me; but she doesn't know how I've adopted them—here—[*she touches her heart*]. Mrs. Farren and Martin—I'd sell my soul for them.

LOMAX [*softly*]. I don't want your soul.

SHIRLEY [*uncertainly*]. I don't know what you mean.

LOMAX. Don't you? Is there anything a girl doesn't know nowadays? [*He stares down at her. She meets his eyes fearlessly, till with a sudden change of tone he says*] Perhaps—if you don't—I'm glad. Good-bye, Shirley. I'll leave you in peace.

SHIRLEY [*catching his arm*]. You can't go like this.

LOMAX. You wanted me to, just now.

SHIRLEY. But about Martin!

LOMAX. Do you never think of anything but Martin?

SHIRLEY [*catching at his arm*]. I won't let you go!

LOMAX [*caressingly*]. Why, Shirley—Shirley darling—

SHIRLEY [*shrinking away again*]. Not that! [*Roughly*] You can do what you like and go when you like. Do you think I care what happens to you? But you've got to make it right for Martin first.

LOMAX [*coolly*]. Now why on earth should I do that?

SHIRLEY. How can it hurt you? Give me back that paper. He said he'd be straight by July. He's been saving—I know that—I know why, now. Can't you see? One slip, yes! but—he's straightened himself! He's been through something, Mr. Lomax. Think what those months must have been. You couldn't ruin him now. Give me that paper and hold your tongue. Won't you? You're going away. It can't hurt you; but it's ruin for him. Don't you understand?—for Martin it's ruin. Why shouldn't you? What has he ever done to you?

LOMAX [*watching her*]. He owns something I wanted.

SHIRLEY [*catching at the hope*]. Martin does? You shall have it. I'll take it on myself, without consulting him. I know there's nothing of his that he wouldn't authorise—

LOMAX. He doesn't know he's got it. So—nothing doing, Shirley Pryde! [*He turns from her once more.*]

SHIRLEY. No! Stop! Tell *me*. What is it, Mr. Lomax? We'll give you anything to get that paper.

LOMAX. Will you?

SHIRLEY. Say what it is! Why can't you say what it is!

LOMAX. Not here! But if you mean it, little girl—[*she twists uneasily under his touch*] if you like to come and fetch it—you shall have your paper.

SHIRLEY. When shall I come? To-morrow morning?

LOMAX. Sooner than that.

SHIRLEY. Now? But they'll be home any minute.

LOMAX. The night's young.

SHIRLEY. What?

LOMAX. Look! there's my window—with the light in it—across the common. I shan't put it out yet awhile. If you want anything of me—come and fetch it.

SHIRLEY. Do you mean—you can't mean— Oh, you're laughing at me!

LOMAX [*losing all control*]. I mean—I'll have what I want as well as you—for once.

SHIRLEY [*struggling*]. Oh—go away! Hateful! Horrible! [*She breaks from him.*]

LOMAX [*violently*]. Oh, you can't do this, you know. You can't see-saw as you've been doing this last half-hour and not come down with a jerk. What do you suppose I'm made of? I'm a man, aren't I? I've got feelings! I've a heart, haven't I? I'd marry you if I could. I've told you that, haven't I? Can I help it that I've tangled myself up years ago? I tell you, she won't divorce me. She's one of these good women—devil! Once, I tell you—just once I went off the rails. And she won't live with me and she won't let me go!

SHIRLEY. I don't want to hear all this.

LOMAX. You've got to hear it, then. What sort of a time do you think I've had of it? A man's got his feelings, hasn't he? Do you think he's just an animal? Well, I'm not. She's done her best to make me—but I'm not. I'm fed up with these catch-as-can women. I want someone to be fond of. I'm fond of you, Shirley. It's a fact. If you'll come away with me, I'd look after you just as if we were married. I'd be as decent—you don't know all I'd do.

SHIRLEY. Mr. Lomax, you're to stop!

LOMAX. I'll stop when I choose and not before. Now I've made you a good offer, haven't I? Come now—and what's more, I'll throw in this business of Martin—I'll make it right as rain for him. Well, what about it? I've got money to burn. I'll give you the time of your life. Even if you got sick of me in a year or two I'd see you don't go under.

SHIRLEY. Will you stop? Will you stop? What have I ever done that you talk to me like this?

LOMAX. Why, if I don't, it'll be someone else, won't it? Once you're on your own.

SHIRLEY. Oh! will you go?

D

LOMAX. What can you expect—as pretty as you are? Muriel isn't a patch on you. How long do you think she'll keep you here, once she's married, for Martin to compare her to—and you in love with him?

SHIRLEY. It's not true. It's a wicked thing to say.

LOMAX. Why are you on your knees to me, then, to keep him out of jail? Why, he'd have had you any time these five years if he'd not been one of these Parsifals, these Sunday-school men.

SHIRLEY. I think you're mad.

LOMAX. Yes, that's what I am—mad—mad for you, Shirley. How long have I been coming here? Two years, isn't it? Have you ever given me a kind word, a kind look? You didn't like me from the start. I saw that. You took good care I'd see it, and feel it too—you rough-tongued little devil—you cold little—

SHIRLEY. Oh, stop!

LOMAX [*ravaged*]. Shirley—love me a little, and I'll give you anything!

SHIRLEY. Oh, be *quiet !* She'll hear you in her room.

LOMAX. I don't care who hears.

SHIRLEY. No, nor whose hearts you break!

LOMAX. Well, do you care whose hearts you break? Aren't I dirt to you, dirt?

SHIRLEY. Yes, you are!

LOMAX. Well I'll have someone else in the dirt too—if that's all your answer!

SHIRLEY. No! No! It's not my answer!

LOMAX. Isn't it ! You darling! You little beauty!

SHIRLEY. Oh, my God!

CHUSSIE'S *voice is heard in the distance.*

CHUSSIE [*in the manner of Gertie Millar*].

" I am so happy when the moon shines out
This is the moment when I long to shout."

SHIRLEY. It's the others—why are they back so soon?

CHUSSIE [MURIEL's *voice joins in*].

" Skipping ! Hopping ! " [*The tune continues, the words broken with laughter.*]

LOMAX. I shall wait till midnight for you and after that I shall address that paper to the firm, and put it in the post.

SHIRLEY. If you do that—

LOMAX. So make up your mind quickly.

CHUSSIE [*vigorously*]. " While the moon shines brightly in the sky."

He and MARTIN, *with* MURIEL *between them, appear in the window, with linked arms, laughing.*

CHUSSIE. Here we are again !

MURIEL [*freeing her arm*]. Oh don't drag so, Chussie ! [*She drops into a chair.*]

MARTIN. Hullo, Lomax, why didn't you come on ?

MURIEL [*glancing at* SHIRLEY]. Need you ask ?

MARTIN. Decent of you to stay with Shirley—your last evening.

LOMAX. I can't say that it is—yet. I may not get off.

MARTIN [*startled*]. What ?

LOMAX [*curtly*]. It doesn't depend on me.

MURIEL. Oh, give me a drink, someone ! [MARTIN *and* CHUSSIE *attend to her.*] Miss Pryde, you do look fagged. [*Pointedly*] You mustn't let us keep you up.

SHIRLEY [*with an effort*]. I'm all right. Was it a good show ?

MURIEL. Rotten. We came out before the end.

CHUSSIE. Pretty good, I thought.

MURIEL. I hate these spy pictures. I like a proper hero and a happy ending.

SHIRLEY [*quietly*]. It must take some—heroism—even to be a spy.

CHUSSIE. Dirty trade.

SHIRLEY. Oh ! if you did it for money—

MURIEL [*yawning*]. And no uniform—nothing.

SHIRLEY [*continuing her own thought*]. But some of them—they did it for love.

LOMAX. Love, Miss Pryde?

SHIRLEY. For love of something—love of country—

MURIEL. You're not going to be patriotic at half-past eleven at night, are you?

MARTIN [*bitterly*]. Dishonour's dishonour, whatever a man does it for, whatever excuses he makes for himself.

SHIRLEY. Is it? To do a dirty thing for a clean reason? And if you value your clean hands more than anything in the world—and yet you dirty them—for someone—is that dishonourable? Were they dishonoured—the spies in the war? They spied for us, for the people at home—for their mothers and their sisters, and their old folk. It was to save *their* honour, if you come to that. [*Looking from one to the other*] Wasn't it?

MARTIN. I suppose so.

SHIRLEY. Just you think—suppose you were a C3 man—not a good soldier, not strong, not fit for that job—the honourable job—and so you forced yourself to the other thing. And what a life! To sneak about, to lie, to be treacherous to people who had been kind to you! And if you were caught—no justice, no honourable terms! A dirty spy! a dog to be shot! Nothing showy, was it, what they did? They can't say afterwards, like you can, Martin, I was in the last offensive. Or you, Chussie—I was at Suvla Bay. Are their mothers to boast, "He was caught red-handed. He was shot as a spy"? Can't you see what they gave? It's so easy to do noble things. But they did the dirty things. They shamed themselves to keep us clean. "Their honour rooted in dishonour stood"; but do you—dare you—despise them?

CHUSSIE [*tolerantly*]. Oh, of course someone's got to do the dirty work. One knows that.

MURIEL [*lounging in her chair*]. But one doesn't want to meet them, exactly.   I expect they were well paid.

CHUSSIE. After all, you can't call it dirty work so long as they're on the right side.   The Huns were spies, if you like, but ours were Secret Service.   Why, some of them were soldiers.

SHIRLEY. Ah, yes; the men!

CHUSSIE. Well, I mean the men.

SHIRLEY. I was thinking of the women.

MURIEL. Anyway, it's five years ago.   It's nothing to get excited about.   Cigarette, Chussie!

MARTIN [*thoughtfully*]. I wonder if Shirley isn't right.   To do a dirty thing for a clean reason—it might be rather fine.

SHIRLEY [*with unnatural eagerness*]. You *do* think that, Martin? you *do?*

MARTIN. I'm not sure.

MURIEL [*through cigarette smoke*]. I don't see how you can do a beastly thing for a good reason.   It's a contradiction.

SHIRLEY. Well, I read about a woman once, in the war—

MURIEL [*bored*]. Oh, in the war!

SHIRLEY. Her mother—ill, and her—brother—in hiding—and a man knew.

CHUSSIE. A Hun?

SHIRLEY. I suppose so.   Anyhow, he threatened to tell unless she—she—

MURIEL. What?

SHIRLEY. He was a beast.

LOMAX. What did she do?

SHIRLEY [*staring at him*]. What he wanted.

MURIEL. Wherever did you pick up such a ghastly story?

CHUSSIE. What happened to her?

SHIRLEY. She kept him quiet.   She saved her own people.

CHUSSIE. I mean afterwards.

SHIRLEY. I don't know.

CHUSSIE. Killed herself, most likely.

SHIRLEY. I don't think she was a coward.

MARTIN [*with conviction*]. My God! no; she couldn't have been a coward.

MURIEL. Well, I think it's a horrible story. As if any nice woman—

SHIRLEY [*passionately*]. She *was* a nice woman—she *was!*

MURIEL. She couldn't have been. No nice woman would do such a thing.

SHIRLEY. But it saved the people she was fond of.

MURIEL. But such a thing!

SHIRLEY [*stolidly*]. In the war, men gave their—bodies—every day.

MURIEL [*getting up*]. Well, of all the morbid conversations! You've got the movie mind, Miss Pryde. Of course, one knows that horrors happened in the war, but that's four years ago. We've settled down to everyday life again. Things like that don't happen. People don't have pasts and secrets. At least, English people don't. [*As she picks up her cloak, her shawl slides unnoticed to the floor.*]

CHUSSIE [*profoundly*]. Oh, I bet you they have 'em all right. What do you think, Lomax?

LOMAX. I think you're all very young, Chussie.

CHUSSIE. Oh don't rot! What do you *really* think.

LOMAX. I think, Chussie, that we each carry one skeleton to every feast.

MURIEL [*uncomprehending*]. Oh, do you think so?

SHIRLEY [*at breaking-point*]. Oh, what does it matter what Mr. Lomax thinks? Why must we all be asking him? He's like the skeleton himself, I think, standing there, listening and grinning at us behind his hand.

MARTIN [*horrified*]. Shirley!

SHIRLEY. Sneering at us because we're young and don't know what to do, and life's so—horrible!

Together { CHUSSIE. One for you, Lomax.

{ MARTIN [*furious with her*]. Shirley, don't be so vilely rude!   Shut up!

LOMAX. Oh, Miss Shirley didn't mean anything.   We understand each other.

MURIEL [*low-voiced*]. That's your domesticated angel, Chussie!

CHUSSIE [*responding*]. Tongue—what? Why has she got her knife into old Lomy?

SHIRLEY. [*catching at her self-control*]. Oh, but you misunderstood me.   I only meant—he *is* rather a skeleton at a feast when—when—

MARTIN [*angrily*]. When what?

SHIRLEY. He said he was going away to-morrow for good. [*With a little high-pitched laugh*] Rather damping.

CHUSSIE. To-morrow? I thought it wasn't till the end of the week?

MARTIN [*urgently*]. To-morrow? Are you going to-morrow, Lomax?

LOMAX. I shan't know till—later.   But I think so.

MARTIN [*with unspeakable relief*]. Ah-h!

CHUSSIE. Well, give us a ting-a-ling in the morning, if you do, and we'll all come to the station.

MURIEL. It's almost to-morrow now.   Look at the moon.   Nearly down.   Chussie, are you going to run me home? [*Then, as* CHUSSIE *goes out*] Oh, let's go round by the pond!

MARTIN [*proprietary*]. I say, Muriel, isn't it a bit late?

MURIEL. Oh, don't be a prig, Martin!

MARTIN. I only mean—

MURIEL. I'm not married to you yet, you know!

CHUSSIE [*from the outer hall*]. Matches, old chap!   My light's out.
            MARTIN *follows him.*

LOMAX [*going up to* SHIRLEY]. Then it's not good-bye, but—*au revoir ?*

SHIRLEY. Oh !—oh !—

LOMAX [*suddenly catching her to him and kissing her*]. On account, Shirley, on account !

SHIRLEY [*crying out*]. Martin.

> LOMAX *steps out through the window and is gone.*

MARTIN [*re-entering*]. Was that you calling ?   Where's Lomax ?

SHIRLEY. He went—garden—

MARTIN. Look here, Shirley !   What the hell made you so rude to him ?

SHIRLEY. I—I—

MARTIN. One of our guests !

SHIRLEY. He—I—I got upset.   I don't think he thought anything.

MARTIN. And apart from that, I should have thought you'd realise that I didn't want any friction just now with Lomax—just now—just as he's going—

SHIRLEY. Oh, Martin don't be angry with me !   I'm so tired I don't know what I'm saying.   I'm sure he—understood.

MARTIN [*believing her*]. Did he ?   [*Then, with his quick change of mood, affectionately*] Why are you so tired ?   Have you been worrying ?   I say, it's no good *your* worrying.   I oughtn't to have talked to you, I know, but—I can't talk to Mother, and so—

SHIRLEY. Oh, I like you to.

MARTIN [*off at a tangent again*]. Oh, I swear to you, Shirley, if I weather this, I've learnt my lesson.   Never again, Shirley, never again !   It's been hell.

SHIRLEY. You've not told me yet.

MARTIN. I can't talk about it now, old thing.   I will, if I get through.

SHIRLEY. But if you didn't ?

MARTIN [*passionately*]. I've got to !   I tell you I've got to !   I couldn't face—some things.   I'd sooner kill myself.

SHIRLEY [*whispering*]. Martin, you mustn't talk like that!

MARTIN. Oh, it's only to you. Well—night! Oh, what about the lights?

SHIRLEY. Turn them out, will you? I'm just coming.

> *She lights the candles on the table, and moves about, tidying the room. She notices* MURIEL'S *shawl, picks it up and begins mechanically to fold it, her thoughts elsewhere.* MARTIN *turns out the lights, picks up one of the candles, and says, as he goes up the stairs:*

MARTIN. Don't dawdle, old thing. It's late.

SHIRLEY [*whispering*]. O God, I believe in You! Give me some sign!

> MARTIN *tramps down the landing.*

MRS. FARREN'S VOICE. Martin?

> MARTIN *stops, and, turning, opens the door a few inches. A bright shaft of light pours out.*

MARTIN. Awake still, Mother? Got all you want?

MRS. FARREN. Come in, my son.

MARTIN. It's too late, old lady! You go to sleep!

MRS. FARREN. You didn't forget the front door?

MARTIN. I didn't.

> *He shuts the door. Before he can turn to his room she calls again.*

MRS. FARREN. Martin!

MARTIN [*with a hand on the balustrade*]. Hullo?

MRS. FARREN. Did you rake the fire out?

MARTIN. Oh—? [*Considering*] No. [*Leaning over the rail, laughingly*] Shirley, that's your job.

SHIRLEY [*giving it a dreadful meaning as she hurriedly repeats it*]. My job! My job! [*Then, under her breath*] Oh, no, *no!* Martin, I can't!

MRS. FARREN. Has she done it, Martin?

MARTIN. No, but she will. [*Over his shoulder*] Won't you, old girl?

SHIRLEY [*after an imperceptible pause*]. Yes.   I will.

MRS. FARREN [*uneasily*]. Yes, but—

MARTIN [*calling to her as he tramps down the passage to his own room*]. It'll be all right, darling! Sleep well!

SHIRLEY [*the forgotten scarf is still in her hand; she flings it round her as she stares after him.   Then she says passionately*] It shall be all right, darling.   Sleep well!

> *She stands a moment bathed in the strong moonlight from the windows.   Then, with a little gasp of determination, she slips out into the garden, drawing-to the window after her. As she disappears, a church clock somewhere in the distance strikes twelve.*

THE CURTAIN FALLS.

ACT II.

It is a little after eleven o'clock of the following morning. The fire is laid, but not lighted, otherwise the scene is unchanged. MRS. FARREN *is in her corner, knitting.* MARTIN *stands at the window, his hands in his pockets, looking out.*

MARTIN [*addressing the universe*]. Of all the loathsome, beastly times in a loathsome, beastly universe, Sunday morning is the loathsomest.

MRS. FARREN [*cheerfully*]. Why don't you go for a nice brisk walk?

MARTIN. Been. D'you realise, Mother, that this God-forsaken stunt of the post-office slackers keeps us without news practically half the week?

MRS. FARREN. Martin, you do exaggerate Are you expecting any letter specially?

MARTIN. Oh, no. It's only the feeling of being out of touch [*Uneasily*] Such a lot can happen between Saturday and Monday, and with no posts you never know what's going to be sprung on you.

MRS. FARREN. Martin! [*He makes no answer, stands, tapping his foot, staring moodily out of the window.*] Martin!

MARTIN [*would-be sprightly*]. Mamma?

MRS. FARREN [*quietly*]. Why are you sleeping so badly?

MARTIN. How do you know?

MRS. FARREN. I heard you in the night.

MARTIN. You didn't hear me.

MRS. FARREN. Somebody was moving about.

MARTIN. It must have been Shirley after biscuits. I never budged.

MRS. FARREN. All the same, you didn't sleep.

MARTIN [*uncomfortably*]. Not well.

MRS. FARREN [*putting down her knitting and holding out a hand to him with the gesture that one uses to a child*]. Martin!

MARTIN. [*defiantly*]. Mother!

> *She sits, her hand still held out to him, waiting. He won't look at her, yet somehow he ends up by crossing over to her and sitting on the arm of her chair.*

MRS. FARREN. My son, when you were born I made up my mind to be a perfect mother, and never ask questions.

MARTIN [*playing with her hand*]. You've been fairly perfect, old lady.

MRS. FARREN. It's been difficult lately, Martin.

MARTIN. Has it, Mother?

MRS. FAR EN [*quaintly*]. Let me off, Martin!

MARTIN [*with an attempt at a smile*]. What do you want to know?

MRS. FARREN [*gently*]. Whatever you want to tell me.

MARTIN. Oh, I've wanted to, right enough, but——

MRS. FARREN. Tell me, Martin!

MARTIN [*after a pause*]. Well, Lomax has gone, anyway!

MRS. FARREN. Was he to go to-day?

MARTIN. It *was* arranged, but he—he didn't seem sure last night. However, he 'phoned through this morning. Chussie and I saw him off. Lonely job going off like that to the other side of the world. I don't know. I was sorry for him, sitting hunched up in a corner of the carriage, without a soul to care if he stayed or went. Queer chap! Sorry he's gone, you know; and yet—oh, the relief!

MRS. FARREN. Is that how you feel about him?

MARTIN. Oh, I like him as much as ever, only——

MRS. FARREN. Only?

MARTIN. That's the story. I can tell you, now Lomax has gone. At least——

MRS. FARREN [*gravely*]. Tell me all about it, Martin.

MARTIN [*not looking at her*]. Well, you see, Mother—

MRS. FARREN. Yes?

MARTIN [*gulping*]. Mother—I—

MRS. FARREN [*steadily*]. Go on, my son.

MARTIN [*getting up suddenly*]. No, I can't! It's too—I *can't!*

MRS. FARREN. Whatever you've done, Martin, makes no difference to me.

MARTIN. I know. And when it's all over— [*He stops and catches sight of* SHIRLEY *coming down the stairs, wearily, pausing on each step, and stops abruptly with*] Hullo, Shirley! [*She lifts her eyes but makes no answer.*] Oh, I say, Shirley, I brought Chussie back to lunch.

MRS. FARREN. Did you? Where is he?

MARTIN. Down in the garden, stuffing himself with raspberries.

MRS. FARREN. Have we got plenty in the house, Shirley?

SHIRLEY. Yes. [*She drags heavily across to* MARTIN, *carrying a paper in her hand. She holds it out to him and says*] Here!

MARTIN [*not taking it, uninterested*]. What have you got there?

SHIRLEY [*dully*]. I think—the paper you were looking for.

MARTIN [*snatching it from her*]. The receipt? My God! Where?

SHIRLEY [*after an instant's hesitation*]. In your room.

MARTIN. Whenever did you find it?

SHIRLEY [*moving towards the kitchen between each answer*]. About an hour ago.

MARTIN [*wildly excited*]. And you never told me? You knew the state I was in. Shirley, you are the most cold blooded— Haven't you any imagination? To let me be here a whole hour and never tell me! You'd only got to run down a flight of stairs! What are you made of?

SHIRLEY [*stupidly*]. I'm sorry, Martin. [*She goes off to the kitchen.*]

MARTIN [*to himself*]. In my room? But I've turned it upside down twenty times! Shirley! [*She stops dead.*] Where exactly was it? [*She stands a moment dumbfounded.*] Eh? Where was it?

SHIRLEY [*with an effort*]. Under the paper in one of the dressing-table drawers. [*She goes out.*]

MRS. FARREN [*patiently*]. What's it all about, Martin?

MARTIN [*to himself*]. My God, the relief! [*Starting*] What, Mother? Yes, I'll tell you now. [*He flings himself down again beside her.*] Oh, Mother, Mother, you don't know what it's been! I got in a hole—got short—got into debt—

MRS. FARREN. Why didn't you come to me?

MARTIN. Your bit of money? No! But I got myself all tied up.

MRS. FARREN. How much?

MARTIN. It ran into three figures. I'd done a flutter. Lomax's tip. His tips were always safe. He was putting his shirt on it himself, and he was ready to let me in. I'd got hard up—it costs money, you know, taking Muriel about, and flowers and all the rest of the racket! But I swear to you, Mother, if I hadn't been dead certain, if it hadn't been a tip from Lomax himself—

MRS. FARREN. And you lost it, of course! What did you do?

MARTIN. I got hold of—some money—to pay it off with.

MRS. FARREN. Where did you get the money, Martin?

MARTIN. Mother—you wouldn't ever guess, I expect, that I could—that I could—

MRS. FARREN. Was it stolen money, Martin?

MARTIN. It was a security—they lent me money on it. Mother it was just lying locked away in the safe—it wasn't being used— it was only a couple of months till my screw came in. I shall have paid it back in a month. And then—last Monday, I go to my desk for the receipt—gone! I tell you, I nearly went off my head. After that six months of misery, Mother, when I was nearly

straight again!   To be pulled up short!   To lose it as a kid might!
Remember the way you used to bully me for carelessness?   For
that silly trick to come in and wreck it!   Think of it, lying about
somewhere, to give me away!   I nearly tore the office inside out, till
I saw Lomax looking at me.   Then I got panic.   If he guessed!   You
see, I'd used his key—when he said last night he might be kept, I
thought it was all up.   Well, he didn't guess.   He's gone.   It's found.
I can get them out of pawn—put 'em back and—over!   No one'll
ever know.   Well, that's that!   And you can guess how proud of
myself I am.   [*Pause.*   MRS. FARREN *sits with her head in her
hand.*]   Well, Mother?   Mother, say something!   [*Then, as he
watches her other hand hide her face*] Mother!   [*He flings himself
down on his knees beside her*] Mother, you're not to!   I can't stand
it!   Mother!   Please!

MRS. FARREN [*her hands in his; not looking at him*]. It's not
you.   It's myself.   I've failed.   Your father—I ought to have
foreseen—I ought to have guarded.   I've been a bad mother to you,
somehow.

MARTIN.   If you take it like that, you'll drive me mad.

MRS. FARREN.   Hush!   There, there, my son!   there!

MARTIN.   Oh, Mother!   [*His head drops on her hands.*]

MRS. FARREN [*in a low voice*].   Martin!

MARTIN.   Yes?

MRS. FARREN [*strained*].   Your father—wasn't straight.

MARTIN [*startled, staring up at her*].   Mother!

MRS. FARREN.   He wasn't kind to me.   I didn't think I'd ever have
to tell you.   I didn't want to tell you, but—selfish of me—I see now.
If I'd told you, perhaps you'd have thought more.   It's a punishment
to me, but—I did love him, Martin.   I didn't want you not to be—
proud of him.

MARTIN [*sternly*].   What did he do to you?

MRS. FARREN.   He wasn't straight.   Will you remember, Martin?

MARTIN [*he has risen*]. Yes. [*He stoops down and kisses her. She clings to him for a moment. Then he turns away from her and walks to the window, and stares out in silence for a moment, before he turns and says abruptly*] What do you want me to do about this?

MRS. FARREN. If you tell them now—will they—prosecute?

MARTIN. I imagine so.

MRS. FARREN. You're paying it back.

MARTIN. Yes, I'm paying it back, you see.

MRS. FARREN [*watching him with intense anxiety*]. I can't judge for you. I mustn't.

MARTIN. It would be the end of my life here. I'd lose Muriel. I'm paying it back.

CHUSSIE'S VOICE [*in the distance*]. Get out! Get out, I say!

CHUSSIE, *somewhat heated, appears in the window, with a cabbage-leaf in one hand and the other beating the air.*

CHUSSIE. Mrs. Farren, Martin's a slacker. You've got more wasps to the square inch than any garden in the row! [*Dodging*] Get out!

MRS. FARREN. There *is* a nest near the raspberry-canes!

MARTIN. Yes, I've been meaning to see to it.

CHUSSIE [*sucking his hand*]. Oh, it's all right, old chap; I've got rid of them for you.

MRS. FARREN. What, all the wasps?

CHUSSIE. No, all the raspberries. [*He deposits a cabbage-leaf in* MRS. FARREN's *lap.*] You like the yellow ones, don't you? [*Over his shoulder, to* MARTIN] Get me a blue-bag, old thing.

MARTIN [*rousing himself to laugh*]. Get it yourself.

CHUSSIE. Mrs. Farren, is that a way to treat a visitor when he's been stung by the family wasp? How can I go looting a strange kitchen?

MRS. FARREN [*twinkling*]. It wouldn't be the first time, Chussie.

CHUSSIE. Oh, that was before Shirley's day. I'm afraid of Shirley when she's cooking.

MARTIN [*lifting his eyebrows*]. Afraid of Shirley?

CHUSSIE. Well, she's a bit "hands-up-or-I-fire," isn't she?

MARTIN [*amused*]. Shirley! Why, she's as mild as milk!

CHUSSIE. Well, I'd rather stand up to Muriel any day of the week.

MARTIN [*lightly*]. You're cracked.

CHUSSIE. No, stung. Mrs. Farren, make him get me a blue-bag.

MARTIN. Lord!—anything for a quiet life. [*He strolls out.*]

CHUSSIE [*triumphantly*]. How's that for strategy? I wanted to get you to myself. Isn't he a quaint old innocent? Swallowed every word.

MRS. FARREN [*putting her knitting aside and shaking out a new skein*]. Hens will peck, Chussie, if you hustle their chicks.

CHUSSIE. Oh, no, you won't. [*He kisses her hand and steals a raspberry at the same time.*] But wasn't he comic just now about Shirley and Muriel? He doesn't know a thing about women. I'll hold that for you—shall I? I'm an expert on jumpers. [*He enskeins himself elaborately.*] That's what I wanted to talk to you about.

MRS. FARREN. Jumpers?

CHUSSIE. No, women.

MRS. FARREN. Any particular woman?

CHUSSIE. Did you see how I led up to Muriel just now? Pretty subtle I thought; and proves my point. Between ourselves—you know I'm only speaking for their good, don't you?—I don't consider he understands Muriel.

MRS. FARREN. Don't you, Chussie?

CHUSSIE. You heard what he said just now, comparing her with Shirley. Well, do *you* think Shirley's as mild as milk? Oh, she's quiet enough, but—I don't know—quiet people scare me. Now Muriel—fuss and fume, if you like, but you do know where you are. Oh, I admit she needs managing, but Martin—he just calls her an

E

angel, and leaves it at that. He doesn't know anything about her.
Now I tell *you*, Mrs. Farren, Muriel's got a temper.

MRS. FARREN. So I've guessed.

CHUSSIE. But he hasn't guessed, you know. He thinks she's a
saint. It's very hard luck on her, always having to hold herself in.
Wearing. If you ask me, I don't think she will much longer. I
think that they're blowing up for a storm, and Martin hasn't even
the sense to tap the barometer.

MRS. FARREN. Are you the barometer?

CHUSSIE. Well, I don't pretend I couldn't give him a tip or two.

MRS. FARREN. It's most disinterested, Chussie.

CHUSSIE. Oh, you always rot a chap. I say, let me wind for a
change! [*The transfer accomplished, he continues*] I *did* wonder if
I'd keep quiet, but you can't call it going behind his back to talk to
you, and all I can say is—I know Muriel, and I know when a thunder-
storm's on the way.

MRS. FARREN. Not the first time you've had to act as a lightning
conductor, eh?

CHUSSIE. Well, I don't want to see Martin a sort of blasted oak.
I say, let's drop metaphors, shall we? I can't keep it up.

MRS. FARREN [*solemnly*]. It is a strain. [*They look at each other
and begin to laugh.*] Well, what is it, Chussie? Out with it. I
won't bite you.

CHUSSIE [*winding*]. Mrs. Farren—!

MRS. FARREN. Chussie!

CHUSSIE. Well, of course you know I adore you. I always have.
[*She laughs.*] It's funny, I always do get on with older women.

MRS. FARREN. Is that a testimonial to you or to them?

CHUSSIE [*waving it aside*]. Look here, if I tell you something—
will you tell me something? Absolute confidence, of course.

MRS. FARREN. Well?

CHUSSIE. Well—[*dreamily*] Muriel's Muriel. [*Then, hastily*] And

Martin's a dear old thing, of course; but when it comes to their getting married to each other, well, frankly, I'm against it.   Are you shocked?

MRS FARREN. Not unduly, Chussie.

CHUSSIE. There, you see!   One can *talk* to an older woman.

MRS. FARREN. So you don't think—it would be wise— ?

CHUSSIE. Well, do *you* think they're suited?

MRS. FARREN. Well, if you won't give me away, Chussie, I don't think they are.

CHUSSIE. I knew you didn't.   I can always tell.

MRS. FARREN. Can you, Chussie?

CHUSSIE. Yes—always could, with women.   I don't do anything, you know—it just comes over me.

MRS. FARREN. Sort of gift!

CHUSSIE [*innocently*]. Yes.

MARTIN [*returning*]. Here you are, blast you!   Shirley had to make one.   [*He throws him the blue-bag and sits on the table, swinging his legs.*]

CHUSSIE. Thanks.   [*Pause.*]   You needn't wait, Egbert.   We'll ring.

MARTIN [*with a sour chuckle*]. I like your cheek !

CHUSSIE. Shut up!   I'm talking to your mother.   If you'd got any sense, you'd get out the garden chairs.   I'd have done it for you if I hadn't had the raspberries to see to.   Always the helpful little gentleman.

MARTIN [*indulgently*]. Fool !

CHUSSIE. Well, Muriel will have to sit on the grass, then, if she comes round ; and if you don't know that Muriel won't sit on the grass in a frock that matters, well, you've something to learn, then, that's all.

MARTIN. Muriel ?   She's spending the day at the Burgs.

CHUSSIE. Oh, no, she isn't.   She's got a head.   She got me to leave a note for them.   It's no joke living next door to Muriel ; you get all the dirty work. Here, that reminds me—got one for you. Catch!

MARTIN. Look here, Chussie, it's the limit! Why didn't you give it me before?

CHUSSIE. Stay me with blue-bags! I forgot.

MARTIN [*reading*]. What's all this about a spill last night?

CHUSSIE [*airily*]. Oh, didn't I tell you?

MARTIN. She wants me to come round at eleven. I say!—and it's past twelve. Chussie, it's a bit thick. [*He dashes to the telephone and unhooks the receiver*] Give me 347 Hat as quick as you can.

MRS. FARREN. A spill, Chussie? Muriel wasn't hurt?

CHUSSIE. Lord! no; she fell on me. Rather a lark, really. We had to leave the old 'bus in Uncle Purdie's front garden and tramp. Didn't matter. Lovely moon. Didn't get home till two.

MARTIN. Well, I won't have it, d'you hear! [*Into the 'phone*] Yes, I want to speak to Miss Hanbury, please. Farren! Yes. [*Then to* CHUSSIE] If you can't look after Muriel—

CHUSSIE. Calm yourself, old dear! She's wiped my eye already.

MARTIN. What? Oh! Oh, thanks. [*He hangs up the receiver*] She's gone out. Say she's probably coming round here.

MRS. FARREN. Better go and meet her.

MARTIN. Yes. Where's my h·t? [*He picks it up and goes off hastily.*]

CHUSSIE [*gravely*]. I say, I do hope she's not coming round here.

MRS. FARREN. Why, Chussie?

CHUSSIE. Look here, Mrs. Farren; something happened last night—rather queer. That's what I've been leading up to.

MRS. FARREN. Last night?

CHUSSIE. I *did* think I'd smoothed her down. I did my best, but if she's coming round here—

> There is a sound of voices.

MRS. FARREN Listen!

CHUSSIE [*scrambling to his feet*]. That's Muriel! Oh, lord she's brought her mother.

MRS. FARREN. What's been happening, Chussie?

CHUSSIE [*evasively*]. I'm afraid we're going to *have* our row.

> MARTIN *returns, escorting* MURIEL *and* MRS. HANBURY, *a shorter, fatter, flabbier version of* MURIEL *herself, but with well-meaning manners and a faint suspicion of a cockney accent.*

MRS. FARREN [*helping herself with a hand on* CHUSSIE'S *arm as she rises*]. Why, Mrs. Hanbury—how nice!

MRS. HANBURY. Now, you mustn't blame me, Mrs. Farren. Murie would bring me along.

MRS. FARREN. Quite right.

MARTIN [*in answer to an unheard remark*]. But, darling, the brute never gave me your note. I thought you were booked till tea-time.

MURIEL [*coolly*]. I changed my mind. How do you do, Mrs. Farren?

MARTIN. As if I wouldn't have been round like a shot!—you ought to have rung me up. Wasting a morning—

MURIEL. Don't fuss, Martin. I came because I wanted to. My shawl—I left it here last night.

MARTIN. I could have run round with it.

MRS. FARREN. Shirley will have put it away, I expect.

MARTIN. I'll ask her. [*Going to kitchen to call*] Shirley!

MURIEL [*crisply*]. I'd just as soon ask her myself, thank you.

MARTIN. Oh, if you want to see her—

MRS. FARREN [*pleasantly*]. I'm afraid she's in the middle of cooking the dinner.

MRS. HANBURY [*gushing*]. Fancy hat, now! Do you hear that, Murie!

MARTIN [*pained*]. If Muriel wants Shirley, Mother, surely she can knock off for a moment. [*Calling*] Shirley! Shirley!

SHIRLEY [*within*]. Coming!

MARTIN [*turning back and down to* MURIEL]. I say, darling, what's all this about a spill?

MURIEL. Last night? [*Coolly*] It was rather a lucky spill.

MRS. FARREN. Not even shaken?

MURIEL. Chussie looked after me. Did he tell you we weren't home till past two?

CHUSSIE [*quickly*]. Didn't tell 'em anything.

MURIEL [*ignoring him*]. Did Chussie tell you who we met?

CHUSSIE [*uncomfortably*]. We didn't, Muriel. As if one could possibly tell!

MRS. FARREN. They're very mysterious, aren't they, Mrs. Hanbury?

MRS. HANBURY [*nervously*]. As long as she don't drag *me* in—

SHIRLEY [*entering, and hesitating as she sees the visitors*]. Good morning, Mrs. Hanbury. Good morning, Muriel. [*Then, as she rubs her hands on her apron*] I'm so sticky, I oughtn't to shake hands.

MURIEL [*deliberately*]. I'm not so keen to shake hands, thanks!

MARTIN [*amazed*]. Muriel!

CHUSSIE [*fidgeting*]. I say, Muriel!

MRS. HANBURY. Now, Murie dear, you did promise me—

MRS. FARREN [*calmly*]. Have you two silly girls quarrelled?

MURIEL [*disdainfully*]. Oh, she knows what I mean all right.

SHIRLEY. I—

MURIEL. Look at her! Of course she does.

MRS. HANBURY [*to* SHIRLEY]. She's just a little put out, my dear, you borrowing her shawl. Not that I'd have minded, but Murie is so particular with her things.

MARTIN [*bewildered*]. What's all this?

SHIRLEY. I—don't know what they mean.

MRS. HANBURY [*half apologetic, half patronising*]. She oughtn't to have left it behind, as I told her. You give it her, and we'll say no more about it.

MARTIN [*to* CHUSSIE]. Do *you* know what they mean?

MURIEL [*sharply*]. Of course he does. He saw her too. It's no use wriggling, Chussie; you know you did.

MRS. FARREN [*with ominous composure*]. Perhaps you'd better tell me just what is the matter, Muriel.

MRS. HANBURY. Oh, Mrs. Farren, they will have their little jealousies.

MURIEL. Jealousy? It's nothing to do with me. Chussie's quite as ready to tell you.

CHUSSIE [*desperately*]. Here! I won't!

MURIEL [*to* CHUSSIE]. If you don't back me up, I'll never speak to you again. I'm only asking you to tell the truth.

MARTIN [*beginning to get angry*]. What's the row, Chussie? Out with it!

CHUSSIE [*cornered*]. Why, it was only—coming home—someone came by us, running through the mist—and Muriel fancied—

MURIEL. Fancied!

CHUSSIE. You know, old thing, it had come over misty.

MURIEL. Misty or not, I knew her, and so did you.

MARTIN. Who on earth are you talking about?

MURIEL. Shirley Pryde, of course! And Chussie knows it.

CHUSSIE. I swear I don't. How could I, with her face all muffled up?

MURIEL. Yes, in my shawl! my new Spanish shawl! The shawl you gave me, Martin. Don't I know my own shawl?

MRS. HANBURY. Oh, yes, Mrs. Farren, it's quite true. She came straight in to me and told me. Very annoyed her father was, to be woke up like that.

MURIEL [*virtuously*]. Well, I thought Mother ought to know. I thought you all ought to know.

MARTIN [*bewildered*]. Why, Muriel, you're not suggesting—

MURIEL [*mulishly*]. I thought you all ought to know.

MRS. FARREN. Know what, my dear? Better be plain about it.

MURIEL. About the sort of things she does behind all your backs.

MRS. FARREN. Shirley, my child, it's very absurd, but I think you'd better explain.

MURIEL. Oh, she'll have an explanation all right.

SHIRLEY [*they have made a half-circle round her*]. I couldn't sleep—so I went out.

MRS. FARREN [*backing her*]. Of course. I heard the stairs go.

SHIRLEY [*gathering courage*]. Just for a walk. I may have picked up Muriel's wrap, just without thinking. I—I'm sorry.

CHUSSIE [*airily*]. There you are, Muriel!

MARTIN [*between resentment and sentiment*]. And, really, my darling, I don't know why you should go for Shirley like this.

MURIEL [*unmoved*]. Will she get me my shawl, please? [SHIRLEY *turns, without a word, to the drawer of the sideboard, and searches in it.*] And when she's given it back, ask her, someone, why she was running about like a mad thing at two o'clock in the morning, and what gate she came running out of! [SHIRLEY *swings round, the shawl dropping from her hand.*]

MARTIN [*furiously*]. Muriel!

MURIEL [*letting herself go*]. Ask her! Ask your immaculate Shirley Pryde! Your paragon of the virtues that you're always crying up to me! Ask her where she spent the night!

MRS. HANBURY [*anxiously*]. Now, Murie! Murie!

MURIEL [*violently*]. Oh, I'm sick and tired of all this virtue and holiness—this domesticated saint that you're always crying up at me! Shirley this! and Shirley that! Shirley's so reliable! Shirley's so quiet! Shirley's so economical! I don't know what we'd do without Shirley!

SHIRLEY [*crying out*]. Oh, it's not fair!

MURIEL [*beside herself*]. Look at her! Isn't she a dear little quiet thing? Housewifery and domesticity and all the silly rot! As if

I didn't see through it! She's a fast little cat, that's what she is, and it's about time you knew it, Martin!

MRS. FARREN [*with dignity*]. Mrs. Hanbury, I think you'd better take your daughter home.

MRS. HANBURY [*nearly weeping*]. Oh, they won't let us interfere, Mrs. Farren. They manage their own affairs now-a-days, the young people. Oh, she's lost her temper, I don't deny. She gets it from her Aunt Marian. But, between you and I, Mrs. Farren, Martin *has* rather held up his sister—

MURIEL [*furiously*]. She's not his sister!

MRS. HANBURY. That's it—that's the trouble, Mrs. Farren—between you and I.

MARTIN [*he has got himself well in hand, but he is very angry*]. Sister or no sister, Muriel, you'll jolly well apologise to Shirley, and to my mother too!

MURIEL. Oh, will I?

MARTIN. I can't believe it of you. I've never seen you like this. You knock me all of a heap. Just because you find another girl doing something that you don't know the reason of—

MURIEL [*with a laugh*]. It's easy to guess, my dear innocent!

MARTIN. —you jump to imagining—I don't like to consider what you're imagining. It's not decent.

MURIEL. I don't need you to teach me decency, nor Shirley Pryde, either! I don't go to a man's rooms in the middle of the night.

MARTIN. A man? What man?

CHUSSIE. I say, Muriel, hold on!

MRS. FARREN. You ride with a man in the middle of the night, my dear.

CHUSSIE [*outraged*]. Oh, but, Mrs. Farren, I say—

MRS. FARREN. I think no more evil of her, Chussie, than I ask her to think of another girl.

MARTIN [*in swift aside*]. Oh, yes, and as to that, Mother, I told Muriel she might.

MURIEL. Told me I might ! I like that ! Did you tell your demi-semi sister that she might ?

MARTIN [*taking a step towards her*]. Muriel, you're to stop talking like that about Shirley.

SHIRLEY [*slowly*]. I don't care what she says, Martin.

MURIEL [*on her like a flash*]. No, but you don't deny it.

MARTIN. She's not got to deny it, not to Mother or me ! I'm not going to insult her by asking her to.

MRS. FARREN. That's right, my son.

MURIEL. It's queer that she doesn't deny it, all the same.

SHIRLEY. I—

MARTIN [*aside*]. You be quiet, Shirley. [*Continuing*] Whatever the silly business means, it's not your affair, Muriel, and I won't have you rude to her.

MURIEL. But she can be as rude to me as she likes, I suppose !

MARTIN. I never heard her.

MURIEL. To listen to you one wouldn't think it was me you were engaged to !

MARTIN [*in a low voice, appealing to her*]. Muriel, are you bent on making things impossible ?

MURIEL [*flinging up her chin*]. It had got to come to a head. I'm not going to have that girl teaching me my business when we're married.

MARTIN [*doggedly*]. And I'm not going to shut my own folk out of my own house when we're married.

MURIEL. It's them or me, Martin.

MARTIN. It seems to me you want to turn me into a cad.

MURIEL. I don't care. You've got to put me first, right or wrong.

MARTIN [*stubbornly*]. I'm not going to round on Shirley.

MURIEL. Well, if that's your choice—

MARTIN. It's no question of choice.

MURIEL [*whirling round on* SHIRLEY]. I wish you joy of my leavings. Come along, Mother.

MRS. HANBURY [*grievously*]. I'm all upset, Mrs. Farren! What you must think— !

MARTIN. But, Muriel, it's impossible! You can't mean—

MURIEL. I'm done with you, Martin Farren! [*As she goes out*] Chussie!

CHUSSIE [*between two loyalties*]. Well—er—I say, Mrs. Farren—

MRS. FARREN. I know, Chussie. But you'd better go. Good-bye, Mrs. Hanbury. [*She calmly shakes hands with the agitated lady.*] See Mrs. Hanbury out, Martin.

MRS. HANBURY [*going*]. What a thing to happen! And on Sunday morning!

MARTIN [*as he holds open the door, to* CHUSSIE]. But, look here—

CHUSSIE. Too rotten, old man! But you leave her to cool down. 'Sure you, I know 'em! [*The three go out.*]

SHIRLEY [*she gives one wild glance towards the door, then rushes to* MRS. FARREN, *with imploring outstretched arms*]. Aunt Lucy! Aunt Lucy! Don't let him find out! I did go! Of course I did!

MRS. FARREN. For him, my girl?

SHIRLEY. Well, of course, for him! Of course! Oh, don't let him guess!

MRS. FARREN [*reassuringly*]. Go upstairs! I'll settle things.

SHIRLEY [*despairing*]. You can't. You won't be able to. He's grown up all of a sudden.

MRS. FARREN. Go upstairs!

       As SHIRLEY *turns to go,* MARTIN *comes back into the room and sees her.*

MARTIN [*gravely*]. Wait a moment, Shirley!

MRS. FARREN [*for the first time in the play a little hurried and uncertain*]. She's thoroughly upset. You must let her be quiet.

MARTIN [*authoritatively*]. I'm sorry. She can be quiet afterwards.

SHIRLEY. There's the dinner—Harness—

MARTIN. Dinner can be late for once. There's something I've got to know.

MRS. FARREN [*curiously losing her calm manner, the more* MARTIN *asserts himself*]. Martin dear, this isn't the moment—

MARTIN. It won't take five minutes. Shirley!

SHIRLEY [*meekly*]. Yes, Martin?

MARTIN [*with a half-smile*]. I don't want to seem unkind, but to put it crudely, old girl, what have you been up to?

SHIRLEY [*almost voiceless*]. Nothing, Martin.

MARTIN [*frowning*]. That's nonsense. [*He hesitates, awkward, then makes a dash at it*] Naturally, I'm not paying any attention to that beastliness of Muriel's, but—there's something.

SHIRLEY [*voicelessly*]. No.

MARTIN [*not unkindly, but reasoning with her*]. I don't think you're telling me the truth.

SHIRLEY. I am telling the truth.

MARTIN [*hardening*]. Well, I'm sorry—I don't believe you.

MRS. FARREN [*anxiously*]. Martin! Martin!

MARTIN. Look here, darling, there's no need to worry you. I—I'd rather like to talk to Shirley by myself.

MRS. FARREN. Shirley won't mind my hearing, Martin.

MARTIN [*lowering his voice*]. Mother dear, you don't know how to deal with these things. Honestly. One can talk to—one's own age. You leave her to me ! She'll tell me.

MRS. FARREN [*gently*]. Martin, I assure you she only wants leaving alone. Muriel was enough to upset anyone.

MARTIN [*bitterly*]. I know. You needn't rub it in.

MRS. FARREN [*thinking she has gained her point*]. Well, then—

MARTIN [*stubbornly*]. It isn't only Muriel. Can't you see, Mother, that she's in some sort of a hole, and that she's afraid to tell us?

[*To* SHIRLEY] Now, look here, old girl! I'm pretty fond of you. And if we aren't brother and sister, I've always felt just as if we were. And what I want to say is, if you've got yourself into any silly mess, don't you be afraid of Mother and me. We'll help you out. Only we must know what you've been up to. We can't have people going about like—like Muriel, saying poisonous things.

SHIRLEY [*turned for an instant*]. Oh, it's my fault you've quarrelled!

MARTIN. Well, tell me the facts, and maybe we can still put it right.

SHIRLEY [*her face setting again*]. There's nothing.

MARTIN [*beginning to get annoyed*]. Oh, nonsense! What did you go to Landsdowne Road for at two o'clock in the morning?

SHIRLEY. I couldn't sleep. I went for a walk.

MRS. FARREN [*quickly*]. It *was* a hot night.

MARTIN [*pinning her down*]. Why not on the Common? Why to Landsdowne Road?

SHIRLEY. I don't know. [*Breaking out*] Oh, it's no business of anyone what I do!

MARTIN [*more kindly*]. I think it is, while you're with us. Oh, of course I know what's happened—

SHIRLEY [*shrilly*]. No—no!

MARTIN [*to his mother*]. Of course she's shielding someone. She's been chaperoning some idiot of a girl. Who does she know in the Landsdowne Road besides Lomax? You heard what Muriel said—she came out of one of the gardens.

SHIRLEY. I didn't! I didn't. It's my own affair.

MARTIN [*putting a hand on her shoulder*]. Shirley, can't you trust us?

SHIRLEY [*gasping*]. I can't. You'd never understand.

MARTIN. I should, Shirley. [*He waits for an answer, but none comes. Suddenly he makes up his mind*] Mother, shall I tell her —about me?

Mrs. Farren [*lowering her head*]. If you choose, Martin. [*She sits down, looking old and worn.*]

Martin. Shirley— [*She looks up at him.*] If I told you that— that I—wasn't the sort of person you thought me—that I wasn't worried, as I told you yesterday, just over business, but because I'd done something pretty bad—pretty beastly mean—would that make you trust me more to understand—trust me to—to let you down lightly?

Shirley [*passionately*]. It wasn't your fault. It was a trap from the start.

Martin. What? What do you mean by that? You know about it?

Shirley [*appalled by the slip*]. I didn't mean anything.

Martin [*shaken*]. Mother, did you hear her? There's something behind this.

Mrs. Farren [*rousing herself into her old manner*]. Can't you see she's on the verge of hysterics?

Martin. I don't care. I *will* know. Who told you about me?

Shirley. No one.

Martin [*savagely*]. Oh, don't lie!

Mrs. Farren. Martin! Martin!

Martin. Well, why can't she tell the truth? Did you tell her, Mother? No, of course you didn't. But no one else knows, except— Lomax? [*Struck*] Has Lomax guessed anything? Did Lomax tell you?

Shirley [*catching at it as a plausible explanation*]. Yes, yes, that was all. Last night. He was here a little while. It was nothing, Martin, only—I—I was worried—and I talked to him.

Martin [*jarred*]. About me?

Shirley. Only just a little.

Martin. He must have thought it pretty queer from you— My goodness, Shirley! I thought I could have trusted you! You might have roused all his suspicions.

SHIRLEY. No, no, Martin! It's all all-right for you.

MARTIN. What did he tell you?

SHIRLEY. Oh—I don't know any more.

MARTIN. Did he know about me?

SHIRLEY. Yes.

MARTIN. He *did* know? And yet he's gone—without giving me away. My goodness! pretty decent! I wonder how he knew.

SHIRLEY [*too quickly*]. Oh, from the receipt. [*She checks herself.*]

MARTIN. He knew I'd lost it?

SHIRLEY [*trying to correct the blunder*]. I mean I told him.

MARTIN. What?

SHIRLEY. That I'd found it, I mean.

MARTIN. You said you didn't find it till this morning.

SHIRLEY [*blankly*]. Did I?

MRS. FARREN. Martin, this isn't leading anywhere.

MARTIN [*dangerously*]. I think it is. So you found that receipt last night?

SHIRLEY. I—I must have.

MARTIN [*swiftly*]. Then why didn't you tell me after Lomax had gone?

SHIRLEY [*helplessly*]. I—I don't know.

MARTIN. You knew I was crazy with worry.

SHIRLEY [*eagerly*]. It was too late. You'd gone to bed.

MARTIN. But I thought you found it in my room? Didn't you find it in my room, Shirley?

SHIRLEY [*cornered*]. I—I don't know! Oh, leave me alone! I'm so tired that I don't know what I'm saying. I've got to see to—

MARTIN [*merciless*]. You must know where you found it.

SHIRLEY [*wildly*]. I don't *know*, I tell you! I picked it up somewhere. Aunt Lucy!

MARTIN. And what did you mean just now by saying it was all a trap?

SHIRLEY. I—

MRS. FARREN [*pitifully*]. Better tell us, Shirley.

SHIRLEY [*pulling herself together for a fresh effort at escape*]. Yes, I'll tell you. Of course I'll tell you! [*With a little laugh*] Such a fuss!—there's nothing to it. Mr. Lomax—he talked to me— only—oh, Martin, he isn't what you thought. He told me he'd been jealous of you, and so—

MARTIN [*bewildered.*] Jealous?

SHIRLEY [*correcting herself*]. Oh, in the business—only in the business. [*With another laugh*] What else should make him jealous?

MARTIN [*not heeding*]. Lomax? Jealous? You don't mean that Lomax was fond of Muriel?

MRS. FARREN [*with a twisted smile, under her breath*]. Muriel!

SHIRLEY [*quickly*]. No, no! Only business. You got on so. He's a hateful man, Martin. Oh, Martin, he's a horrible man! So, when he came across that receipt in your desk—

MARTIN. It was Lomax who had it? Lomax?

SHIRLEY. Oh, it's all right! I talked to him. He gave it back to me. That's all, Martin dear. Dear Martin, that's all!

MARTIN [*to* MRS. FARREN]. I haven't got this straight.

MRS. FARREN [*with a last effort to regain her authority*]. I think it's quite clear, Martin. Shirley seems to have found out the truth and persuaded Mr. Lomax—

SHIRLEY. That's it.

MRS. FARREN. It's very good of her, and very plucky.

MARTIN. Then why couldn't she tell me so last night?

SHIRLEY. I—

MRS. FARREN [*finally*]. I think we can leave it now.

MARTIN [*uninfluenced*]. I want to get things straight. When did he give you that receipt?

SHIRLEY [*glibly*]. He posted it. [*Checking herself, quickly*] I mean—he was going to post it—

MARTIN [*thinking it out*]. He didn't give it you before I went to bed, so—

SHIRLEY [*frenzied*]. No, Martin! No, Martin, no! Aunt Lucy— can't you stop him!

MARTIN [*relentlessly*]. So Muriel was right. They did see you in the Landsdowne Road. It was his gate you were coming out of.

SHIRLEY [*wailing*]. Oh, I only went to fetch it.

MRS. FARREN. Martin, can't you leave ill alone?

MARTIN [*dominant*]. I *will* have the truth. You and Lomax— Lomax and you! What's been happening? What have you been arranging behind my back?

SHIRLEY [*piteously*]. Nothing! Nothing!

MARTIN [*realising things*]. You've been lying to me the whole time! What is it between you and Lomax? What's this secrecy? Is he in love with you? Are you in love with him?

SHIRLEY [*shivering*]. He's horrible to me.

MARTIN. Yet you went to his rooms?

SHIRLEY. He made me. He said he'd ruin you. He wouldn't give it to me unless—

MRS. FARREN [*warning her*]. Shirley, Shirley, d'you know what you're saying?

SHIRLEY. I—!

MARTIN. D'you mean—?

SHIRLEY [*at the end of her strength*]. Yes.

MARTIN. My God!

SHIRLEY [*in a last desperate rally*]. It's my own affair what I do.

MRS. FARREN [*going to her*]. You poor child!

MARTIN [*stopping her*]. Mother! Do you understand what this means?

MRS. FARREN. I'm afraid I do.

MARTIN. Shirley? Our Shirley? Lomax? It can't be true. [*He goes to* SHIRLEY *again and puts his hand on her shoulder*] Shirley, it's not

F

true, is it, old girl? [*She clutches at his hand with both hers, and dragging it down to the table, buries her face on it.*] No, of course not! It's hysteria, Mother. The way girls are sometimes.

MRS. FARREN [*shaken*]. D'you think so? It's possible.

SHIRLEY. Can I go away now—somewhere—quiet?

MRS. FARREN [*gently*]. Yes, my dear, yes! You shall do whatever you like.

MARTIN [*equally gently*]. Yes, Shirley dear, in a minute. But you must clear this up for us, because—Lomax—you and Lomax— I've got to see Lomax, you know, to get things put straight for you.

MRS. FARREN. Lomax is out of the way.

MARTIN. He can't get out of my way, if it's true. Shirley, this affair between you—has it been going on long?

SHIRLEY [*she lifts her head to stare at him—then, suddenly rising, she cries out*]. Oh, how dare you!

MARTIN. What?

SHIRLEY [*wounded to the heart*]. How *can* you!

MRS. FARREN. She's been terrorised, can't you see?

MARTIN. But they must have had an affair.

SHIRLEY [*frantic, forgetting everything*]. No, no! Never! It was only for you. I had to, Martin! He said he could send you to prison.

MARTIN [*appalled*]. Are you putting this on to—me?

SHIRLEY. You said last night you'd throw yourself under a train.

MARTIN. You knew I was just talking—the way one does.

SHIRLEY [*piteously*]. I was afraid for you.

MARTIN. You mean to tell me that you did this ghastly thing—

SHIRLEY. It was the disgrace—it would have killed Aunt Lucy. I had to stop it.

MARTIN [*dangerously quiet*]. I see! You couldn't trust me to look after my own mother. Well, I suppose you can say you were justified in that. Say it, if you like. It's your hour.

SHIRLEY [*urgently*]. It was for both of you. If you'd been found out, he said you'd be done for! You'd never get a job again.

MARTIN. Well, and if it were so—

SHIRLEY [*in desperate appeal*]. I couldn't let it happen. Martin, can't you understand? Ask yourself—what would you have done if you'd been me. You two are all I've got.

MARTIN [*still with the same ominous calm*]. I see. And so you've settled it all. Is that it? Our troubles are over—the trouble that I've brought on my mother and myself—you've put it all right for us—

MRS. FARREN [*watching him*]. Martin, be careful!

MARTIN [*unheeding*]. We're to shut our eyes, and say thank-you and settle down again, is that it?

MRS. FARREN. Martin!

MARTIN. That's *your* side of it. Now I'll show you mine. Now I'll ask *you* something! How dared you do this to me?

SHIRLEY. *For* you!

MARTIN. For *me?*

SHIRLEY. For you! For her! It was such a great trouble to come upon you!

MARTIN. You say you've done this for us—

SHIRLEY. The wicked thing for the good reason, Martin. Can't you see?

MARTIN [*convulsed*]. Yes, I see. I see very clearly what you've done. I wasn't proud of myself, anyway. I didn't think I was much. But now—you've put such a shame upon me that I can't breathe. What right had you to shame me so? What right had you to smear my life with your ghastly—charity? I'll bear my own burdens. Did I ask you to take over my sins? Is that what you've always thought of me—that I'm the sort of man to let a woman—buy me off? How dare you make me into such a foul thing!

MRS. FARREN. Martin! Martin!

MARTIN. You've branded me. Do you think I can ever forget it? It's beyond pardon—beyond belief!

MRS. FARREN. Martin, have you the right to judge?

MARTIN. D'you say that to me, Mother? My own mother? Then I tell you, I'll buy back my rights. [*He takes the paper from his pocket, and with it in his hand turns from them to the door.*]

MRS. FARREN. Martin! Martin! What are you doing? Don't act hastily! That won't make things right.

MARTIN. It'll begin to.

SHIRLEY. Where's he going?

MARTIN. To make a clean breast of this business—to take what they give me.

SHIRLEY. No, no! Aunt Lucy, stop him!

MARTIN *goes out.*

MRS. FARREN. Let him go. He has his soul to save.

SHIRLEY. But what shall *I* do? It's all gone for nothing, what I did! I did it all for nothing!

MRS. FARREN. You can't tell yet, my child. You can't tell yet!

THE CURTAIN FALLS.

ACT III.

SCENE I.

The scene is the same as it was just two years ago. It is late in the afternoon. THE DOCTOR, *a brisk youngish man, is standing at the foot of the stairs, his note-book and pen in his hand, speaking over his shoulder to* SHIRLEY, *who is closing the door of* MRS. FARREN'S *bedroom behind her.*

THE DOCTOR [*scribbling as he talks*]. No, I wouldn't put her to bed. On the contrary, get her out! Bath chair. Plenty of fresh air. But no exertion, you understand. No excitement. No household worries. No jumping up suddenly if ,the telephone rings and that sort of thing.

SHIRLEY. Oh, I've always been very careful. [*She has come down the stairs and they both take a step or two into the room.*]

THE DOCTOR [*pulling off a page*]. This won't hurt her, after meals : three times a day. By the by, when was she overhauled last ?

SHIRLEY [*all through the scene she is very quiet and practical in manner*]. Not for a couple of years. You see, old Dr. Matheson died. He'd attended her for years—an old friend. And you know—new faces. It's only lately I got alarmed and—

THE DOCTOR. Ah ?

SHIRLEY. It's the breathlessness. It *is* worse, though she won't have it. So I persuaded her to see you.

THE DOCTOR. I wish I'd seen her sooner.

SHIRLEY. Oh Doctor—you don't think it's—

THE DOCTOR [*interrupting*]. You're a—daughter, eh ? Niece ?

SHIRLEY. I look after her.   I'm no relation.

THE DOCTOR [*obviously assuming from that that she is merely a nurse*].   Ah!   Has she got any relations?

SHIRLEY. A son.

THE DOCTOR [*meditatively*].   I'd rather like a chat with him.

SHIRLEY. He's abroad.

THE DOCTOR [*with a jerk of his head towards the bedroom door*]. Misses him, eh?

SHIRLEY. Yes.

THE DOCTOR. Hm!   Likely to be home soon?

SHIRLEY. We—she doesn't know his plans at the moment.

THE DOCTOR. Could you get him home?

SHIRLEY. Not to live.

THE DOCTOR. Pity!   Not for a year or two?

SHIRLEY [*coldly*]. There are reasons.   He—he lost his job over here.   She wouldn't want him to come back for good.

THE DOCTOR [*musing*]. Farren—Farren— Didn't I hear something—ah yes!   Young scamp, eh?   [*With another jerk of his head*] Lived on her, didn't he?

SHIRLEY [*angrily*]. He didn't!   Never!   That's one of the lies they tell.   He never let her help him even when he— Why, he sends her home money!   He works like a nigger!   Oh, it's *like* people to hit him when he's down!   Who told you?

THE DOCTOR. Patients will talk.

SHIRLEY, Who?

THE DOCTOR [*smiling*]. That's confessional.

SHIRLEY [*pouncing*]. Do you know Chussie Hare's wife?

THE DOCTOR. Hare—Hare?

SHIRLEY. She was Muriel Hanbury.   Just had a baby.   I expect you attended her.   Well, what did she tell you—that he'd been in prison?   Yes, that's true.   But the rest's lies.   Live on his mother! He's not that sort of man.

THE DOCTOR. Prison, eh? Poor woman! That accounts for a lot.

SHIRLEY. But it's two years ago now.

THE DOCTOR. Long sentence?

SHIRLEY. Six months.

THE DOCTOR. Has she seen him since?

SHIRLEY. No, he went abroad at once.

THE DOCTOR. Does she worry about him?

SHIRLEY. She'd never let you know if she did.

THE DOCTOR. You'd better write and tell him to come home pretty soon if he wants to see her.

SHIRLEY. Doctor! As bad as that?

THE DOCTOR. Precaution. You see Miss—Miss—?

SHIRLEY [*mechanically*]. Pryde.

THE DOCTOR. Miss Pryde—you can never tell with these heart cases. Keep her quiet and she may live another two years.

MRS. FARREN [*opening the door of her room*]. Shirley! Shirley! Has Dr. Rodson gone yet? Won't he take his tea with us, now we've kept him so long?

THE DOCTOR [*picking up hat and gloves*]. Don't you fret about me, Mrs. Farren. I'm due at the other side of the Common by five. [*He moves to the door accompanied by* SHIRLEY.]

MRS. FARREN. Well, if you're sure—

THE DOCTOR [*talking himself out*]. Well, Miss Pryde, get that made up and I'll come in towards the end of the week. [*They go out.*]

MRS. FARREN *comes out of her bedroom and slowly and cautiously descends the stairs, holding the rail. She crosses the room and sits down a little shakily in her accustomed place by the fire. After a moment she gives a little amused, impatient glance at the open door and with a shrug picks up the cards lying beside her and begins shuffling, humming to herself as she does so.*

MRS. FARREN. " What's this dull town to me?

Robin's not here!

What was't I wished to see?

What wished to hear?

Where's all the joy and mirth—"

SHIRLEY [*in the doorway, reproachfully*]. Aunt Lucy! To come downstairs by yourself! What is one to do with you?

MRS. FARREN [*briskly*]. Oh, is that the latest? Mayn't walk about my own house now! And what else did he say, pray?

SHIRLEY [*evasively*]. I've got to go down to the chemist.

MRS. FARREN. It didn't take him a quarter of an hour to say that. Don't tell me! I heard you conspiring.

SHIRLEY [*behind her chair*]. Now, Auntie!

MRS. FARREN [*smiling*]. Out with it!

SHIRLEY [*her arms round her, leaning her cheek against the soft grey hair*]. I'm to take great care of you, and you're to take great care of yourself.

MRS. FARREN [*looking straight in front of her, her hands folded in her lap*]. How long does he give me?

SHIRLEY [*the clasp of her hands tightening*]. Auntie dear! Auntie dear!

MRS. FARREN [*after that instant's stillness, as brisk and whimsical as ever*]. Don't you come Auntie-dearing me! You think yourself very grown up all of a sudden, don't you? Chit! Here I've bath'd you and smacked you and taught you manners and—

SHIRLEY. Loved me!

MRS. FARREN [*putting up a hand to the two that are holding her*]. Yes, I've loved you. And then you have the—the neck—as Martin would say—to talk over me and my symptoms with a strange man! [*With a change of tone*] I'm worse, aren't I?

SHIRLEY [*her voice failing her a little*]. You're not frightfully fit.

MRS. FARREN. I could have told him that. [*Stamping her foot*] Don't *cry*, you silly child !

SHIRLEY. I'm not—I—

MRS. FARREN. Well, of course you'll miss me ! But take it from me, my dear, it'll be no bad thing for you to be on your own. Rouse you. One can be too indispensable. [*With a sigh*] I'd like to have seen Martin first though.

SHIRLEY [*quickly*]. Oh—I'm writing to-day.

MRS. FARREN [*pouncing*]. Oh, then it *is* merely a question of months?

SHIRLEY. No, no ! If we're very careful—no worries, no excitement—

MRS. FARREN. Oh, dull ! [*At a tangent*] Shirley, if you go into mourning, I'll haunt you !

SHIRLEY. Aunt Lucy ! Please !

MRS. FARREN. Hate black. So does Martin. Shirley, if—if Martin and I—miss each other—

SHIRLEY [*confidently*]. He'll come. Don't you worry !

MRS. FARREN. You don't know where to write to. It's three months since he wrote.

SHIRLEY. Three months and a week.

MRS. FARREN. Don't you go blaming him !

SHIRLEY. I don't, but— Oh, why didn't he come back to us, to you, when he first got out. It was so cruel.

MRS. FARREN. He just couldn't. I understood.

SHIRLEY. Because—of me ?

MRS. FARREN. Because of himself. He'd got to make good first. I understood. He knew I understood.

SHIRLEY. If he'd cared as we care—

MRS. FARREN. Men have their work. They don't realise how long the days can be.

SHIRLEY. Oh—so long !

MRS. FARREN. With nothing to do but—knit—and take medicine and—[*with a half laugh*] tell the cards.

SHIRLEY [*she is sitting by now on the low stool beside* MRS. FARREN'S *chair, her elbows on her knees, her chin in her fists*]. Do you remember—that time we told the cards?

MRS. FARREN. I remember. And you see—it's all come true.

SHIRLEY. It hasn't all come true.

MRS. FARREN. It'll come. I know what you're thinking of.

SHIRLEY. You don't.

MRS. FARREN [*quoting*]. "Clubs. The dark woman. And a marriage card between them! Do *you* know any dark woman?"

SHIRLEY [*rising and pacing restlessly up and down*]. Aunt Lucy, don't torment me!

MRS. FARREN [*dreamily*]. I'd like to meet her, before I die. There's a lot I could tell her about my son.

SHIRLEY [*in a low voice*]. There's no such woman. [*But she draws nearer.*]

MRS. FARREN [*as if to herself*]. I'd tell her—to be patient, without seeming to be patient—

SHIRLEY. That's hard.

MRS. FARREN. To give—yet always seem to take.

SHIRLEY. That's hard too.

MRS. FARREN. To be hard when you ache to be gentle—to laugh at your own tears—

SHIRLEY. That could be learned.

MRS. FARREN. Never to give him all he wants.

SHIRLEY [*with a little cry of pain*]. Oh—!

MRS. FARREN. But to love him, Shirley, whatever he.does.

SHIRLEY [*low*]. I'll tell that woman—if ever I get a chance.

MRS. FARREN [*with a complete change of tone*]. But above all, Shirley, tell her to stand up for her rights.

SHIRLEY. Rights, Aunt Lucy? Rights? What's the good of rights?

MRS. FARREN. I may be Victorian, but I *approve* of the women of to-day. They're full-grown citizens. If Martin comes back— grown—he won't want a mother to bully him, or a sister to run his errands. He'll want a partner: a woman with rights of her own. You think that over!

SHIRLEY. Why do you say all this to me?

MRS. FARREN. It's a message I give you—a message to Martin and the woman he marries.

SHIRLEY. " The dark woman—"? [*She tries to laugh lightly.*]

MRS. FARREN. Tell them—that they were made for each other, and that his old mother knew it and sent them her blessing.

SHIRLEY [*restlessly*]. Why do you talk like this—just because a silly doctor—?

MRS. FARREN. It wasn't the doctor. I knew all he could tell me. [*Leaning back and closing her eyes*] I'm tired, Shirley.

SHIRLEY [*all concern, forgetting herself*]. Well, of course! My fault! I let you talk when I ought to have got you your tea. Wouldn't you like it in the garden? It's so hot to-day.

MRS. FARREN. I'm so tired, all of a sudden.

SHIRLEY. He said you were to have all the air you could. We'll have it on the lawn. I'll get out the bath-chair, shall I?

MRS. FARREN. Can't Harness—?

SHIRLEY [*going*]. It's only in the tool-shed.

MRS. FARREN [*uneasily*]. I wish you'd let Harness— [*But SHIRLEY has gone. Left alone MRS FARREN turns restlessly in her chair, stretches out her hands to the cards, and begins another patience. She murmurs*] Two on the three, three on the four— [*Then, as she gets more engrossed, she hums to herself once more, very softly, the words hardly audible*]

" But now thou'rt gone from me,
Robin Adair!

But now thou'rt gone from me,
Robin Adair ! "

[*Considering*] Queen on the Jack!
" Yet him I love so well
Still in my heart doth dwell— "
[*Triumphantly*] And *that* for the rubbish heap!
" Oh, I can ne'er forget— "
[*A postman's knock interrupts her. She calls sharply*] Harness !
[*The knock is repeated. She touches a little bell*] Harness ! Harness !
[*Then, as* HARNESS *comes in, with a touch of excitement*] It's the post-
man, Harness! He's waiting. He wants something. Be quick !
[*She sits listening intently while* HARNESS *hurries through to the outer
door and returns with a letter in her hand.*] Well?

HARNESS. A foreign letter, Ma'am ! Understamped. There's to
pay. [*She gives it to her.*]

MRS. FARREN. It's from Mr. Martin ! [*Then, as she tears it open
with a fumbling hand*] My purse is on the table. Take what you
want ! [*Then, as* HARNESS *takes up the purse*] From Mr. Martin,
Harness.

HARNESS [*beaming*]. There, Ma'am ! [*She goes out once more.*]

MRS. FARREN [*reading, radiant*]. Oh ! Oh ! [*Then, as* HARNESS
*returns once more, leaving the door open, she turns to her, shaking
with excitement*] Call Miss Shirley ! He's coming home, Harness.
He's coming home. Miss Shirley—in the garden—to come to me !
Mr. Martin's coming home. [*She absorbs herself in her letter again
as* HARNESS *goes out through the French windows, commenting on it
with little smiles and nods, and tiny laughs between her words*]
Well—yes— Bless him !— Yes, of course !—dear boy—the dear
boy ! [*and so puts it down (it is very short) with a long sigh of
happiness. She closes her eyes a moment, then some sound that no one
else hears rouses her again. She turns*] What's that? [*No answer,
but she still listens, her eyes on the door.*] Harness ! Wasn't that a

knock? [*Then, in growing excitement*] Shirley! Listen! Oh, can't one of you go? It's Martin! [*Half rising*] I tell you it's Martin! Open the door! I tell you it's his step. Open the door, Shirley! Run! [*She is on her feet by now, wild with excitement, watching the door. Her movement has brought her in a line with the window and the afternoon sunlight is full on her face. Suddenly her tense expectancy changes to a very lovely smile. She opens her arms wide and says in a deep, sweet voice*] Well? Well, Martin? You're late, my son! [*She stands so a moment, then, without any sound, collapses into her chair as* SHIRLEY *comes running in from the garden, crying joyously.*]

SHIRLEY. A letter? A letter from Martin? Aunt Lucy, Harness says there's a letter from Martin! [*Then, getting no answer, astonished*] Aunt Lucy! [*But when she reaches the chair and sees what she sees, she cries out in a harsh, terrified voice*] Harness! Harness! Harness, come here a minute!

HARNESS [*in the doorway, startled*]. Why, Miss—?

SHIRLEY [*sharply*]. Come here! Come here! I don't know what's happened. She doesn't move! [HARNESS *hurries to her side as the curtain falls.*]

ACT III.

SCENE II.

*The scene is the same as in the preceding Acts, but there are no flowers,
and one or two little personal possessions of* SHIRLEY'S *that, as
you now realise, have always brightened the room are missing.
The Shakespeare calendar has left a light oblong on the wall-
paper, and the drawing of* MARTIN *has been removed from its
frame. The silver on the sideboard has also disappeared, and
the room altogether is unnaturally tidy. A strapped bundle of
rugs and a suit-case stand in a corner, with an umbrella laid
across them. It is early afternoon. Outside it rains steadily,
audibly, though it clears off as the scene progresses, and the end
of the act is played in bright sunshine.* HARNESS *is helping an*
OUTSIDE PORTER *to carry a small trunk down the stairs.*

HARNESS [*anxiously, on the lowest step*]. Mind the paint, porter!
PORTER. Right.

      HARNESS *drops one end and he shifts it on to his shoulders.*
HARNESS. Got it?
PORTER. Right. [*He goes out.*]
HARNESS [*calling after him*]. She'll meet you at the barrier for
the seven o'clock.
PORTER. Right!

      The outer door slams after him, and HARNESS *turns back
into the room as* SHIRLEY *comes hastily down the upper
passage and leans over the banisters. She is in travelling
clothes and carries a hat and dust cloak over her arm.*

SHIRLEY. What was that? Who was that?

HARNESS. Only the outside porter, Miss.

SHIRLEY [coming down the stairs]. Oh, of course!

HARNESS. Your trunk'll get fair soaked in this downpour. You ought to have waited, as I said, and took it along in a taxi.

SHIRLEY [as she lays her hat and cloak on a chair]. Shall you take a taxi when you go to your new place?

HARNESS. That's quite different, Miss!

SHIRLEY. I don't see it. We can't either of us afford taxis, anyway.

HARNESS. Then I suppose it does mean a new place for me, Miss?

SHIRLEY. I'm afraid so, Harness. Of course, it'll depend on Mr. Martin's plans.

HARNESS. I can't see 'im hanging on 'ere with the poor lady gone, not if you go too, Miss. Not but what I wouldn't stay on, willing—

SHIRLEY. I know you would, Harness. But I don't know his plans.

HARNESS. I couldn't undertake meals, not what you call meals, but I'd get him his breakfast.

SHIRLEY. Well, I'll tell him, Harness, and he can talk to you.

HARNESS. Oh, you ask him, Miss, and then you tell me one way or the other. [A knock.] That'll be Mr. Martin, won't it? Shall I go to the door, or will you?

> SHIRLEY, with a dumb gesture, signs her to the door as the knock is repeated. She stands at the table, with her hands lightly clasped, waiting; but when the door opens, it is CHUSSIE who comes in, breathless and in some agitation, the rain dripping from his hat.

SHIRLEY. Chussie! Why, I haven't seen you—

CHUSSIE [shaking hands pleasantly, but with weightier matters on his mind]. Oh, yes, how d'you do—so pleased and all that—but, look here, you know, I've got Muriel in the porch. Can she come in a minute?

SHIRLEY [*stiffening*]. If she cares to.

CHUSSIE [*confidentially*]. Oh, she's kicking at it, too, all right. But we've got the pram, you see. First time the kid's been out. And look at the weather! Got caught. Can't see a taxi anywhere.

SHIRLEY. Of course. Wheel it into the hall while I ring you one.

CHUSSIE [*horrified*]. It? Here, I say, it's a he! [*Shouting*] It's all right, Muriel; come on!

MURIEL's VOICE [*fretfully*]. Chussie! Shouting like that!

SHIRLEY [*at the telephone*]. 31, please. [*Then, watching the bustle in the entrance hall, she says with a little smile*] Come in, Muriel; don't be so silly.

> MURIEL *enters, cross and uncomfortable. She is not so pretty as she was, is stouter and much less carefully dressed.*

MURIEL. It's not my fault. I said it would rain. But Chussie always will know best. It's very kind of you, Miss Pryde.

SHIRLEY. Take off your mackintosh and give it a shake.

MURIEL. But the carpet!

SHIRLEY. It won't hurt it.

MURIEL. So extraordinary to find oneself here again; but you see, the rain was blowing right on to his face.

SHIRLEY. Oh, the baby!

CHUSSIE [*enthusiastically*]. I expect you're longing to have a peep. I'll bring him in here.

MURIEL. No, no, Chussie, he's asleep!

CHUSSIE [*disappointed*]. You might let her just have a look at him.

MURIEL. He's such a sensitive child. Strangers upset him.

SHIRLEY. Don't bother, Chussie! [*Then, into the telephone*] Yes? Well, I've been waiting a good five minutes. Have you got a taxi? Send it round to Friars' End Road, will you? No. 23. Thanks! Good-bye. [*Then turning*] Do sit down, Muriel!

MURIEL [*uncomfortably*]. I'm sure I wouldn't have come in, but Chussie—

SHIRLEY [*pleasantly*]. Why shouldn't you come in and shelter?

MURIEL. Oh, I don't know—so awkward meeting Mrs. Farren.

SHIRLEY [*quietly*]. Didn't you know that Mrs. Farren was dead?

MURIEL. What—dead?

CHUSSIE [*shocked*]. Oh, I say!

MURIEL. Chussie, you might have *told* me!

CHUSSIE [*deeply concerned*]. I didn't know. I had no idea—I say, I am sorry. When?

SHIRLEY. About three weeks ago.

MURIEL. I wish we'd known—flowers or something—

CHUSSIE. I say, does *he* know?

SHIRLEY. Martin? I wrote, of course. The letter will have caught him at New York.

CHUSSIE. Why? Not coming back, is he, old Martin?

SHIRLEY. I'm expecting him this afternoon.

MURIEL [*pursing her lips*]. What? Here?

SHIRLEY [*looking at the clock*]. He said about three.

CHUSSIE. Muriel, we'd better get a move on.

MURIEL. Yes, he won't want to run into us.

CHUSSIE. Isn't that our taxi stopping at the gate? [*He moves to the window.*]

MURIEL [*to* SHIRLEY]. Hope so. It's so awkward.

SHIRLEY. Why?

MURIEL. Will he know about me and Chussie?

SHIRLEY [*perfunctorily*]. Oh, *that!*

MURIEL. I don't want to add to his troubles.

CHUSSIE [*at the window*]. There's a man getting out.

SHIRLEY [*in an entirely expressionless voice, but her hands clench themselves*]. That will be Martin, I expect.

MURIEL [*embarrassed*]. Oh, damn!

CHUSSIE [*opening the window*]. I say, taxi! Keep that taxi!

G

MURIEL [*fumbling with her waterproof*]. Miss Pryde, I think we'll slip into the next room.

> *But the knock at the door is followed instantly by* HARNESS'S :

HARNESS. Oh, Mr. Martin !

CHUSSIE. That's torn it !

HARNESS. She's in the sitting-room, Sir.

> MARTIN *enters. He is a good deal changed—has "filled out " and lost his boyish look. He looks tired, but tanned and healthy. He enters with an eager gesture of the hands, and then stops dead.*

MARTIN [*blankly*]. Oh, visitors !

CHUSSIE [*rushing at him, effusively*]. Hullo, old thing ! Hullo ! Glad to see you. Going at once, you know. Only blew in for a second. Ripping to see you and all that. And now—now we're clearing out. Muriel !

MARTIN [*pleased*]. Why, Muriel ! Did you come—Muriel ? That was ripping of you !

CHUSSIE [*quickly*]. Oh, yes, you know, don't you ?—my wife !

MARTIN [*smiling*]. What ! You two ? Congratulations !

CHUSSIE [*embarrassed*]. Yes, married, you know. Son and heir in the hall—pram. Mustn't keep him waiting.

MARTIN [*going up to* MURIEL]. Muriel ! [*She tosses her head.*] You look so fit, but—what is it ? Different, somehow. Not a bit what I remember. I'm glad that you and Chussie—

MURIEL [*stiffly*]. Good-bye. We mustn't keep you.

MARTIN. Good-bye. [*He puts out his hand. She passes him, ignoring it.*] What ? [*Then, understanding*] Oh ! All right !

CHUSSIE [*anguished*]. Oh, I say, Muriel ! [*Shaking hands with* MARTIN *in grieved apology*] I can't help it, old man. They're like that. You wait till you're married! [*Then, at the door*] Buzz round later, what? [*He goes out.*]

MARTIN *stands staring after them.*

SHIRLEY. I'm sorry, Martin. They came by accident. I couldn't get rid of them.

MARTIN. That's all right! [*He comes down into the middle of the room.*]

HARNESS [*putting her head in*]. Miss Shirley! Miss Shirley! Will he have tea?

SHIRLEY [*worried*]. Oh, no, no! [*She hurries to the door, obviously to get rid of her.*]

HARNESS. I could make it in a minute. I've got the kettle on.

SHIRLEY [*softly*]. Not now, Harness, not now. I'll ring.

HARNESS. Well, I thought, Miss, a cup o' tea—

SHIRLEY [*edging her into the hall*]. It's nice of you, Harness. A little later. [*The voices cease as the door closes behind them. But in a moment* SHIRLEY *re-enters, saying once more*] I'm sorry, Martin [*He takes no notice. She watches him with intense anxiety for a moment. Then she says again, timidly*] Martin!

MARTIN [*to himself*]. I did think—she would be here.

SHIRLEY [*anxiously*]. But, Martin, you did know?— You got my letter—?

MARTIN. Oh, yes, I got it. But I did think, somehow—that she—that there'd be a feel of her—[*his voice fails*].

SHIRLEY [*strained*]. Old man—old man!

MARTIN. Too silly, when I knew—but somehow I thought all the time—suppose it's not true—suppose she is there—suppose there could be—

SHIRLEY. A miracle.

MARTIN [*with a choking laugh*]. Yes. Against all hope—a miracle.

SHIRLEY. I felt that way once. But that's not the way things happen. There aren't any miracles.

MARTIN. No.

SHIRLEY. Only folly and [misery—and then death comes. That's all.

MARTIN. That's all. I knew it when I came in. And yet, as I came down the road I told myself a silly tale, that it was all a dream —these two years—and your letter and all—and that she'd be there, Mother darling, just the same—"Well, my son!" But there's no one. No one but you.

SHIRLEY. No one but me.

MARTIN [*with a sigh*]. Oh, well—! [*He moves restlessly about the room in silence. Then*] Muriel just now—I didn't know her. Was she always—like that?

SHIRLEY. How do you mean?

MARTIN. I thought—I didn't think she'd—turn on one—quite like that.

SHIRLEY. She was always like that, Martin.

MARTIN. Yes, I suppose so. I can't make out why I—[*he breaks off*].

SHIRLEY [*gently*]. She was so pretty—two years ago.

MARTIN. I suppose it was that. Well! she's well rid of me. [*Another pause. Then, without looking at her*] Well, what do we do now?

SHIRLEY [*stiffly*]. I've got one or two things to tell you—business.

MARTIN [*nodding*]. Yes, of course.

SHIRLEY. I've put the house to rights. I've gone through everything, the way she told me to. It's all straight for you before I go.

MARTIN [*politely*]. What are your plans?

SHIRLEY [*equally polite*]. I'm all right. I've got work. I'm going to be a servant.

MARTIN [*startled into looking at her*]. What are you talking about!

SHIRLEY [*unmoved*]. I can do that best. I'm pretty efficient and it's good pay.

MARTIN. I never heard such nonsense!

SHIRLEY [*conclusively*]. That's what I'm going to do.

MARTIN [*reasoning with her*]. But this house, you know—it's up to you to use it. And there's Mother's four hundred—I thought you'd better have half that.

SHIRLEY. Did you, Martin?

MARTIN [*kindly*]. Truly, you can take it.

SHIRLEY [*inscrutably*]. Truly, can I take it?

MARTIN [*with an immense effort at cheerfulness*]. You needn't worry about me. Where d'you suppose I'm going on to, of all places in the world? Chili. I've got the offer of a permanent job.

SHIRLEY. So you're running away again?

MARTIN [*brought up short*]. What do you mean?

SHIRLEY [*bitterly*].

> "From excellent intentions that didn't turn to good,
>   From ancient tales renewing"—

Don't you know it? It's "The Song of the Broken Men."

MARTIN. "Broken"? That's where you're wrong. I'm not broken. I've been a damn fool. I've been a wicked fool, if you like—and I've smashed up my life over here. But I'm not broken. I'm making my life again. Better. I'm not broken.

SHIRLEY. Then you'll come back again, Martin, some day?

MARTIN. No, I don't think so.

SHIRLEY [*nodding vaguely*]. No.

MARTIN. Why should I? There'll be nothing to come back for, now. I shall cut absolutely loose. I think it's wisest, don't you?

SHIRLEY [*very quietly*]. Oh, yes! much the wisest. Well, good luck, Martin, wherever you go. [*With a sudden hardening of manner*] But I won't take your money.

MARTIN [*overriding her in all kindness*]. Oh, yes, that'll be all right. I'll fix that all up before I go.

SHIRLEY [*breaking out*]. How *can* you be so brutal to me!

MARTIN [*amazed and rather hurt*]. Shirley!— Why—why, I only want to know that it'll be all right for you. Can't you see I've got a duty?

SHIRLEY [*subsiding again*]. Oh, is that it?

MARTIN [*generously*]. D'you think I don't realise all you must have done for Mother all these last months? Do you think I'm not grateful?

SHIRLEY [*not looking at him*]. Have I ever asked you for— gratitude?

MARTIN. It's not a question of what you ask. It's a question of what's up to me to do. I know how good you've been, and it was up to me to come back and see that you were all right. That's all I came back for—that and—[*he stops—awkwardly, angry with himself for being tongue-tied*].

SHIRLEY [*impassive*]. Well, you see I'm all right, don't you?

MARTIN. You don't let me finish—you never let a person finish!

SHIRLEY [*meekly*]. Sorry.

MARTIN. I wanted—I want to know— [*He looks to her for help, but she does not help him. He begins again*] Mother—you were with her all the time, weren't you?

SHIRLEY. It was like it always was.

MARTIN. Your letter just said—just said—it wasn't a letter: it didn't tell me anything—only the bare fact.

SHIRLEY. It might not have reached you. I didn't think you'd want more written down in a letter that other people might open.

MARTIN. No—no—of course.

SHIRLEY [*with difficulty*]. I didn't know, either—that from me—

MARTIN [*ingenuously affectionate*]. I couldn't ask anyone but you, Shirley.

SHIRLEY [*wilfully misunderstanding*]. No, you couldn't ask Harness, I suppose.

MARTIN [*amazed at her lack of feeling*]. How could I bear to ask anyone but you? Of course I understood about your letter. That's why I came back—to see you. I thought you'd tell me things.

SHIRLEY. I'll tell you anything you want to know.

MARTIN. I want to know—everything.

SHIRLEY [*without emotion*]. It was just three weeks ago. We'd been talking—a long talk—and she'd got a little excited. And then your letter came while I was out of the room. Harness gave it to her. Harness said she seemed so pleased. And she said it was good news, and Harness was to find me at once. So Harness did. But when I came back into the room, she—she—[*her voice plays her false*].

MARTIN. I see.

SHIRLEY [*under control again; softly*]. Just like being asleep.

MARTIN [*at last*]. I—see. I— It's a weight off my mind, Shirley; I was afraid of dreadful things. You know—pain—or a fall—or a shock. [*Passionately*] But if it had been a shock, it would have been two years ago, wouldn't it, Shirley? It would have been when it all happened. [*She doesn't answer.*] Shirley! Shirley, why don't you say yes?

SHIRLEY [*harshly*]. The doctor said it was a sort of shock. It was the letter—knowing you were to be home so soon—she sort of—died of joy.

> *He stares at her a moment, his face working. Then he breaks down utterly, sitting at the table, his head on his arms.*

SHIRLEY [*she has risen, and passed swiftly behind him, her hands moving over him; under her breath*]. Martin—Martin—don't! You mustn't, Martin! Martin, old man! [*She touches his cheek softly, with a stroking gesture of the hand.*]

MARTIN [*stiffening instantly*]. It's all right! [*He gets up abruptly*

and strides over to the window.   She stands looking after him, in
her old frightened, drooping pose, and presently he says] You say
you were talking with her for an hour beforehand?

SHIRLEY. Yes.

MARTIN. Well?   [*She says nothing.*]   What about?

SHIRLEY [*stiffly*]. About you.

MARTIN [*eagerly*]. Were you?   [*With a friendly look at her*]
Well?

SHIRLEY [*always with the same stiff manner*].   We talked about
you.

MARTIN [*encouraging*].   Yes?

SHIRLEY. That's what—we—talked about.

MARTIN [*impatiently*].   Well?

SHIRLEY [*cornered*].   I don't know what you want me to say,
Martin.

MARTIN [*stormily*]. My God, Shirley!   Haven't you any heart
at all?

SHIRLEY [*stubbornly*]. Yes, I have.

MARTIN [*with impatient entreaty*].   *Well* then—*well* then?

>   *She looks at him with the same air of almost mulish un-*
>   *comprehension and says:*

SHIRLEY. I've arranged to go after tea.   Can I do any things
for you before I go?

MARTIN [*breaking out*]. How can you be so brutal to me?

SHIRLEY [*amazed in turn*]. I?

MARTIN [*at full pelt*]. What possesses you?   You've got a devil, I
think.   Don't you know what I'm feeling?   Can't you guess?   Am
I to drag things out of you in cold blood?—all the little things I'm
crying out to hear.   You were with her—you took my place—tell
me what she said and did, the last days!   [*Entreating her*] Don't be
a stone, Shirley.   She talked about me?   She sent me messages?
[*She nods*] What were they, Shirley?   Tell me what she said!

SHIRLEY. No!

MARTIN. What?

SHIRLEY. I can't.

MARTIN. What?

SHIRLEY. I won't.

MARTIN. Are you completely off your head?

SHIRLEY [*stubbornly*]. She left it to me. She said—all the things she was telling me—I needn't tell you if I didn't think right—if I didn't think you'd understand. And I don't. You aren't the Martin she believed in. He doesn't exist. There was just a dream of a boy in her heart—good—kind—and it was him I was to talk to—to tell everything to—not you. You're not Martin. You're just like any other man. You're only thinking of yourself.

MARTIN [*his amazed anger turning into almost comical alarm*]. Shirley! Shirley dear, I think you're ill. You're not yourself. You're worn out, that's what it is. It's all been too much for you.

SHIRLEY. Yes, it's been too much—too much, Martin, and I'm not going to bear it any more. [*She turns from him.*]

MARTIN [*suspicious*]. Where are you off to?

SHIRLEY. I'm going. I don't want to talk to you. I don't want to see you. I want to get away.

MARTIN [*angrily*]. You'll stop here.

SHIRLEY. Oh, don't be melodramatic! [*But she hesitates, all the same.*]

MARTIN. Then don't *you* be! [*He pulls out a chair for her*] Sit down, now. We've got to have this out. You've no right to treat me like this.

SHIRLEY. No, I've never had any rights.

MARTIN. What have I done? You've always been so—

SHIRLEY [*sharply*]. So what?

MARTIN. Such a dear—such a dear old thing—and now, all of a sudden— [*Then, his head up, as a new idea strikes him*] Are you ashamed of me? Is that it? Are you playing Muriel's game? Are you ashamed of me?

SHIRLEY [*with intense bitterness*]. Ashamed? I?

MARTIN. Well then, what is it?

SHIRLEY [*staring in front of her ; in a low voice*]. Martin! Do you remember when we saw each other last? D'you remember that morning—

MARTIN. Don't !

SHIRLEY. —what you said to me here in this room?

MARTIN [*not looking at her*]. What's the good of harking back ?—back to those things? Forget them as quickly as we can.

SHIRLEY. Forget? What do you suppose I've thought of in these last two years—all day and every day—and every night too?

MARTIN. And what d'you suppose I've thought of? Why do you force me to speak of it? D'you think I'm not raw from it still? D'you think I'm not sick and sorry for what I did?

SHIRLEY. And I? D'you think I'm not sorry?

MARTIN. Remember? Haven't you *any* imagination? Can't you think what it's been like—day and night—going over it—wondering how one ever came to be such a fool—such a fool—such a fool ! Oh, but you know it was mostly folly, Shirley. I had the money—it was coming to me—

SHIRLEY [*in her mothering voice*]. Yes, yes, Martin. Of course I know.

MARTIN [*catching himself up*]. Ah ! The old excuse ! I swore I'd never say that again. There's no excuse. None. But you're right. I'm not that boy any more that she knew. It's done something to me—in these two years—Fate—Chance—whatever you choose to call it.

SHIRLEY. Is it just Chance—the way things happen ?

MARTIN. What else? Think ! Quiet people in a quiet suburb—

and a silly fool too hard up to buy a girl flowers. That's where it started. And look where we are to-day! Look what it's done to us—Mother—Muriel—you! What's the purpose of it all, now we're at the end? None, I tell you! It's just the way things choose to happen.

SHIRLEY. Hadn't you a purpose when you—came out of prison?

MARTIN. You know I had. You must have guessed I had! And there you are again—Chance steps in and stops me! What's the good of stamping on a dying rat? That's what Lomax was when I knocked into him at last. And his wife had gone out to him. She opens the door to me. That's the way things happen. What is one to do?

SHIRLEY [*half stretching out a hand to him*]. What you did.

MARTIN. Yes—I came away: laughed at again by—Chance! All the same, I'm not beaten, I tell you that. I'm starting again. D'you think I ought to be hanging my head? I won't. I've paid, Shirley. Two years of thinking of what one's done—it's payment in full for most things.

SHIRLEY [*imploring*]. Yes, it is, Martin, isn't it?

MARTIN [*unheeding*]. I've paid! That's over. Now I'll start again.

SHIRLEY [*changing the key of the scene—as she rises*]. And what about me?

MARTIN. You?

SHIRLEY. I've had two years too—in prison.

MARTIN [*in shocked remonstrance*]. Shirley!

SHIRLEY [*with every sentence intently pursuing and pressing home her meaning*]. D'you say quits to me? Can I start again?

MARTIN [*hesitating*]. I don't know quite—what you're driving at.

SHIRLEY [*painfully*]. You said—that morning—you said I'd put such a shame upon you—

MARTIN [*wincing*]. Oh God, Shirley, can't you let sleeping dogs lie?

SHIRLEY [*relentless*]. You said you'd never forget and never forgive. Have you never forgotten?

MARTIN [*in a low voice*]. I'm trying to.

SHIRLEY. Have you never forgiven?

MARTIN [*lower still*]. I don't know.

SHIRLEY. In those two years were you never sorry for me?

MARTIN. I wouldn't think of you.   There are some things one has to shut out of one's mind.

SHIRLEY [*bitterly*]. So, after all—after all you say—in these two years you've learnt nothing.

MARTIN. That's not true.   You don't understand.

SHIRLEY. It's you who don't understand.   You say you're not going to fail again.   Well, I tell you, you will.   You may not do a foolish thing again—dishonest, if you like to call it that—but you'll do worse—you'll do cruel things.   You've done one already, even in this one hour.

MARTIN. I don't understand you.

SHIRLEY [*with rising excitement*]. I ask you again—do you remember when we saw each other last?   Think back !   And now, to-day, it's the first time that I see you since.   What does it mean to me, do you think, to see you again?   But you don't think of me.

MARTIN. That's not true, Shirley.

SHIRLEY [*riding him down*]. It is true !   Have you given me one personal look—one personal word?   What have you talked to me about, except when I made you?   Yourself and your mother.

MARTIN. Isn't it natural?

SHIRLEY. Isn't it natural to think of me too?   But it's always your mother, your mother !

MARTIN [*aloof*]. I'm not going to brawl with you about my mother.

SHIRLEY. What are you trying to make out?   Didn't I love her too?   You come to me for comfort, but you never think that I could want comfort.   And you come to me for kind words, for some-one to listen to your plans—

MARTIN. I didn't mean to bore you.

SHIRLEY [*passionately*]. You didn't mean to bore me! You can say that to me! And I've been in your house twelve years!

MARTIN. I only meant—

SHIRLEY. What other home have I got? What other friends? Weren't we sister and brother? Whatever there's been between us since, whatever wrong I've done you or you me, when you come back—like this—for the sake of old times you could have been kind— you could have said, "How are you, Shirley?"—and that you'd missed me a little, and that—maybe—you'd write to me sometime, even though she's—gone.

MARTIN [*protesting*]. But I took it for granted.

SHIRLEY. That's it! You take everything for granted. You always have. First your mother and then me.

MARTIN [*getting angry*]. You're not to talk of Mother in the same breath—

SHIRLEY [*facing him*]. You're not to talk of me in the same breath. I'm a woman to myself.

MARTIN [*trying to be patient*]. When you're married, Shirley, and have your own son, then you'll understand.

SHIRLEY [*jealously*]. What'll I understand?

MARTIN. What she gave me—what she was to me—what— Oh! but all that was between us two. I can't talk to you of those things.

SHIRLEY [*wildly excited*]. But *she* could. There's not a word I've said to you she didn't bid me say.

MARTIN. She? She could no more say the things that you've been saying, deliberately, to hurt me— Oh, you don't understand!

SHIRLEY [*on the heights*]. I'm a woman, and I do understand. And she—she knew I did. That's why she trusted me. We were two women together. Not young and old, not wise and foolish—two women together. She's dead, and you're all alone in the world, Martin. But when you get on again, and get rich and successful, and make your life again the way you're going to, still you'll be alone in the world. And if you marry—some other Muriel—still you'll be alone. But remember, you needn't have been! You've lost her, your mother who loved you. But the way she loved you, that isn't lost. I know the way it happens: I've learned it. I know the way mothers love: it comes from the pain, the pain they suffer. I'm the only other woman in the world for you who knows it, the only woman in the world who could have given you her beautiful things. Yes, if I'd loved you, Martin, instead of—hating you, I think—I could have given you—beautiful things. [*She turns as if to go.*]

MARTIN [*stopping her*]. You shan't go! I don't know what you mean.

SHIRLEY [*fiercely*]. No, and that's why I'll always despise you.

MARTIN. You'll take that back! [*He catches her by the shoulders.*]

SHIRLEY [*struggling*]. I won't! Oh, let me go—I don't want you!

MARTIN. You shan't say—" despise "!

SHIRLEY. I do! I will! There! [*She strikes him across the mouth*] Will that show you?

MARTIN. Oh! [*Then, furiously*] You'll stop that, d'you hear! You've done enough to me! I'll teach you to stop that sort of thing! I'll teach you! I'll teach you!

SHIRLEY [*flinging up her chin*]. Teach me, then! [*She stares up at him defiantly, her mouth trembling, her eyes bright with tears.*]

MARTIN [*staring down at her*]. I'll—I'll— [*But as their eyes meet, his face changes, and his grip on her shoulders relaxes, though his hands do not drop; and he says, half whispering*] What is it, Shirley? Shirley, what is it? What's happening to us?

SHIRLEY [*weakly, smiling*]. I think—it's—love.

MARTIN [*with intense passion, in a low voice*]. Shirley! Shirley! Shirley!

SHIRLEY [*triumphantly*]. You love me, Martin! You love me! [*Her arms go round his neck*] And, oh, I love you so!

With a swift movement he catches her close, and they kiss.

MARTIN [*suddenly, holding her away from him*]. Look here! I say! Is that—is this what we've been up against all this while?

SHIRLEY [*between laughter and tears*]. She said so.

MARTIN. Mother?

SHIRLEY. She said—that's what I couldn't tell you, Martin, while we hated each other.

MARTIN. Hate you! *you!* I've loved you all my life. Why, you little fool, weren't we made for each other?

SHIRLEY [*in his arms again*]. Yes, Martin—yes, Martin! That's what she said!

THE CURTAIN FALLS.

January-March, 1922.

PRINTED IN GREAT BRITAIN BY
WOODS AND SONS, LTD., LONDON, N. I.